TEACHER'S PET PUBLICATIONS

LitPlan Teacher Pack™
for
Lord Of The Flies
based on the book by
William Golding

Written by Mary B. Collins

This **LitPlan** for William Golding's
Lord of the Flies
has been brought to you by Teacher's Pet Publications, Inc.

TABLE OF CONTENTS - *Lord of the Flies*

A FEW NOTES ABOUT THE AUTHOR
William Golding

GOLDING, William. William Golding was born in Cornwall in 1911. He attended Oxford where he began as a science major but later changed his major to English literature.

During World War II, he joined the Royal Navy and achieved the rank of lieutenant. He participated in both the Walcheren and D-Day campaigns.

Following the war, he began to teach and write. Some of his works include: *Lord of the Flies, The Inheritors,* and *Pincher Martin.*

INTRODUCTION

This unit has been designed to develop students' reading, writing, thinking, and language skills through exercises and activities related to *Lord of the Flies* by William Golding. It includes twenty-one lessons, supported by extra resource materials.

The **introductory lesson** introduces students to one main theme of the novel through a role-playing activity. Following the introductory activity, students are given a transition to explain how the activity relates to the book they are about to read. Following the transition, students are given the materials they will be using during the unit. At the end of the lesson, students begin the pre-reading work for the first reading assignment.

The **reading assignments** are approximately thirty pages each; some are a little shorter while others are a little longer. Students have approximately 15 minutes of pre-reading work to do prior to each reading assignment. This pre-reading work involves reviewing the study questions for the assignment and doing some vocabulary work for 8 to 10 vocabulary words they will encounter in their reading.

The **study guide questions** are fact-based questions; students can find the answers to these questions right in the text. These questions come in two formats: short answer or multiple choice. The best use of these materials is probably to use the short answer version of the questions as study guides for students (since answers will be more complete), and to use the multiple choice version for occasional quizzes. It might be a good idea to make transparencies of your answer keys for the overhead projector.

The **vocabulary work** is intended to enrich students' vocabularies as well as to aid in the students' understanding of the book. Prior to each reading assignment, students will complete a two-part worksheet for approximately 8 to 10 vocabulary words in the upcoming reading assignment. Part I focuses on students' use of general knowledge and contextual clues by giving the sentence in which the word appears in the text. Students are then to write down what they think the words mean based on the words' usage. Part II nails down the definitions of the words by giving students dictionary definitions of the words and having students match the words to the correct definitions based on the words' contextual usage. Students should then have an understanding of the words when they meet them in the text.

After each reading assignment, students will go back and formulate answers for the study guide questions. Discussion of these questions serves as a **review** of the most important events and ideas presented in the reading assignments.

After students complete reading the work, a lesson is devoted to the **extra discussion questions/writing assignments**. These questions focus on interpretation, critical analysis and personal response, employing a variety of thinking skills and adding to the students' understanding of the novel.

There is a **vocabulary review** lesson which pulls together all of the fragmented vocabulary lists for the reading assignments and gives students a review of all of the words they have studied.

There are three **writing assignments** in this unit, each with the purpose of informing, persuading, or having students express personal opinions. The first assignment is to express personal opinions and be creative: students continue the role-playing scenario begun in the introductory lessons by keeping a daily journal of the things that happen to them and their classmates as they are stranded on a deserted island. The second assignment is to inform: students organize and summarize the information they have read for the nonfiction reading assignment. This serves the double purpose of helping to prepare the students for an oral presentation about the same information. The third assignment is to persuade: students are sent to the island to persuade the boys that they should try to get along better. Students write a persuasive speech to present to a gathering of the boys on the island.

In addition, there is a **nonfiction reading assignment**. Students are required to read a piece of nonfiction related in some way to *Lord of the Flies*. After reading their nonfiction pieces, students will fill out a worksheet on which they answer questions regarding facts, interpretation, criticism, and personal opinions. During one class period, students make **oral presentations** about the nonfiction pieces they have read. This not only exposes all students to a wealth of information, it also gives students the opportunity to practice **public speaking**.

The **review lesson** pulls together all of the aspects of the unit. The teacher is given four or five choices of activities or games to use which all serve the same basic function of reviewing all of the information presented in the unit.

The **unit test** comes in two formats: all multiple choice-matching-true/false or with a mixture of matching, short answer, multiple choice, and composition. As a convenience, two different tests for each format have been included.

There are additional **support materials** included with this unit. The **extra activities packet** includes suggestions for an in-class library, crossword and word search puzzles related to the novel, and extra vocabulary worksheets. There is a list of **bulletin board ideas** which gives the teacher suggestions for bulletin boards to go along with this unit. In addition, there is a list of **extra class activities** the teacher could choose from to enhance the unit or as a substitution for an exercise the teacher might feel is inappropriate for his/her class. **Answer keys** are located directly after the **reproducible student materials** throughout the unit. The student materials may be reproduced for use in the teacher's classroom without infringement of copyrights. No other portion of this unit may be reproduced without the written consent of Teacher's Pet Publications, Inc.

The **level** of this unit can be varied depending upon the criteria on which the individual assignments are graded, the teacher's expectations of his/her students in class discussions, and the formats chosen for the study guides, quizzes and test. If teachers have other ideas/activities they wish to use, they can usually easily be inserted prior to the review lesson.

UNIT OBJECTIVES - *Lord of the Flies*

1. Through reading William Golding's *Lord of the Flies*, students will study human nature and consider the question of whether or not man is inherently good or evil.

2. Students will demonstrate their understanding of the text on four levels: factual, interpretive, critical and personal.

3. Students will consider what it means to be "civilized."

4. Students will study the symbolic images in *Lord of the Flies*.

5. Students will experience making a civilization through a group activity.

6. Students will be given the opportunity to practice reading aloud and silently to improve their skills in each area.

7. Students will answer questions to demonstrate their knowledge and understanding of the main events and characters in *Lord of the Flies* as they relate to the author's theme development.

8. Students will enrich their vocabularies and improve their understanding of the novel through the vocabulary lessons prepared for use in conjunction with the novel.

9. The writing assignments in this unit are geared to several purposes:
   a. To have students demonstrate their abilities to inform, to persuade, or to express their own personal ideas
      Note: Students will demonstrate ability to write effectively to <u>inform</u> by developing and organizing facts to convey information. Students will demonstrate the ability to write effectively to <u>persuade</u> by selecting and organizing relevant information, establishing an argumentative purpose, and by designing an appropriate strategy for an identified audience. Students will demonstrate the ability to write effectively to <u>express personal ideas</u> by selecting a form and its appropriate elements.
   b. To check the students' reading comprehension
   c. To make students think about the ideas presented by the novel
   d. To encourage logical thinking
   e. To provide an opportunity to practice good grammar and improve students' use of the English language.

READING ASSIGNMENT SHEET - *Lord of the Flies*

Date Assigned	Reading Assignment (Chapters)	Completion Date
	1-2	
	3-4	
	5-6	
	7-8	
	9-11	
	12	

UNIT OUTLINE - *Lord of the Flies*

1	2	3	4	5
Introduction	Introduction PV 1-2	Read 1-2	Study ?s 1-2 PVR 3-4	Study ?s 3-4 PVR 5-6
6 Library	**7** Study ?s 5-6 PVR 7-8	**8** Study ?s 7-8 PVR 9-11	**9** Study ?s 9-11 PVR 12	**10** Study ?s 12 Extra Questions
11 Vocabulary	**12** Writing Assignment 2	**13** Speaker	**14** Nonfiction Reports	**15** Writing Assignment 3
16 Film	**17** Film	**18** Discussion	**19** Journals	**20** Review
21 Test				

Key: P = Preview Study Questions   V = Vocabulary Work   R = Read

STUDY GUIDE QUESTIONS

SHORT ANSWER STUDY GUIDE QUESTIONS - *Lord of the Flies*

Chapters 1 - 2
1. Identify:
  Ralph
  Piggy
  Simon
  Jack
  Sam & Eric
  Maurice
  Roger
  "The littluns"
2. How did the boys happen to come to the island?
3. What do the boys have that is the symbol of authority in the society they form?
4. What does the reader learn about Jack when he slashed the green candle buds?
5. Why does Jack hesitate when he lifts his knife to kill the piglet, and what does he promise will happen next time he meets a pig?
6. Who are the hunters, and what is their job?
7. What does a little 'un think he has seen in the forest?
8. How and why do the boys make fire?
9. Why does the boys' plan for rescue fail?

Chapters 3 - 4
1. Although Ralph criticizes the boys for their lack of cooperation, does he bear some of the responsibility for the failures of the group to achieve its goals? Why or why not?
2. How has Jack's personality developed during his stay on the island?
3. Ralph says of Simon, "He's queer. He's funny." What kind of a boy is Simon?
4. After Maurice and Roger destroy the littluns' sand castles, Roger stalks the young boy named Henry. When he begins to throw stones, why does he just throw them near him instead of directly at him?
5. What causes the hunters, who had promised to keep the fire burning, to neglect it and allow it to go out?
6. Why does Jack paint his face?

Chapters 5 - 6
1. How does the author show us that Ralph is finally beginning to face the realities of their existence?
2. Compare Ralph's treatment of the littluns with Jack's.
3. What is Simon saying when he thinks the "beast" may be inside they boys themselves?
4. What do Sam and Eric tell the boys they have seen? What is it actually?
5. Why do Ralph and Jack decide to go find the beast?

Chapters 7 - 8
1. How does Ralph react when a boar comes charging down the path?
2. To what does Ralph's demonstration of his hunting prowess lead?
3. What did the boys see on the mountain top?
4. Why is the action of the story increasingly taking place in the near darkness or in the deep night when only the moon and stars give a little light?
5. How does Ralph's waning confidence in himself show in his words and actions?
6. Although he is not able to get the boys to vote Ralph out of office as chief, Jack manages to overthrow Ralph's authority anyway. How?
7. Jack suggests a way to keep the beast happy. What is it?
8. Describe Simon's strange encounter with the Lord of the Flies.
9. Who or what is the Lord of the Flies?

Chapters 9 - 11
1. What does Simon find when he finally reaches the Beast?
2. What happens to Simon when he returns to the group?
3. As a result of the storm with its high winds and high tides, what happens to the bodies of Simon and the parachutist?
4. What does Jack plan to steal from Ralph and Piggy?
5. What will Jack do if someone interferes with him?
6. What happens to the conch and to Piggy?
7. What are Jack's plans for Ralph?
8. What course of action does Ralph take?

Chapter 12
1. What is Ralph's reaction when he encounters the pig's skull?
2. Driven by fear and hunger, Ralph manages to make contact with Samneric who are standing guard at Castle Rock. Of what do they warn him?
3. In what ways does the tribe try to hunt down Ralph?
4. What or who saves Ralph in the end?

ANSWER KEY: SHORT ANSWER STUDY GUIDE QUESTIONS - *Lord of the Flies*

<u>Chapters 1 - 2</u>
1. Identify:
   Ralph - handsome, athletic, natural leader
   Piggy - very intelligent, physically less than perfect fat boy, a reader and thinker rather than a boy of action
   Simon - poetic, sensitive, loner, rather mysterious boy
   Jack - choir leader, "ugly without silliness"
   Sam & Eric - identical twins later known as Samneric, as if they were one
   Maurice - choir boy as big as Jack, "grinning all the time"
   Roger - secretive, "slight, furtive boy" who later shows a natural tendency towards cruelty
   "The littluns" - name given to the numerous little children of the group

2. How did the boys happen to come to the island?
   These school boys have been ejected from a flaming airplane. It appears no adults have survived the crash.

3. What do the boys have that is the symbol of authority in the society they form?
   The conch shell is the symbol of authority. It shows who is boss and who has the right to speak.

4. What does the reader learn about Jack when he slashed the green candle buds?
   Jack's method of dealing with the world seems to be violent.

5. Why does Jack hesitate when he lifts his knife to kill the piglet, and what does he promise will happen next time he meets a pig?
   Jack's hesitation shows that he must learn to put aside his inhibitions, whether they are learned or natural. He promises that "next time there would be no mercy."

6. Who are the hunters, and what is their job?
   The choir boys have become hunters. Their job is to get food.

7. What does a little 'un think he has seen in the forest?
   He thinks he has seen a "snake-thing" which he later calls a "beastie."

8. How and why do the boys make fire?
   The boys make a fire to act as a signal for their rescue. They use Piggy's glasses as a "burning glass" to start the fire with the sun's rays.

9. Why does the boys' plan for rescue fail?

> The boys did not have a well-thought-out plan. They used too much wood for a small, controllable fire, and they never thought of a way to control the fire to keep it from getting out of hand. Most of their readily-available firewood was burned up, making keeping the fire going much more difficult.

Chapters 3 - 4

1. Although Ralph criticizes the boys for their lack of cooperation, does he bear some of the responsibility for the failures of the group to achieve its goals? Why or why not?

> Ralph is partially responsible for their failures. He has the desire to bring a measure of civilization to the island, but he lacks the competence to do so. He believes life is much like a story book, and that although there will be obstacles, the clever boys will overcome them all, and they will emerge victorious in the traditional, happy ending. Ralph has an idealized view of life and can never actually get a grip on carrying out his plans.

2. How has Jack's personality developed during his stay on the island?

> Jack has degenerated from a superficially civilized school boy to a near animal level. He yearns to kill, yet he too is learning the vast difference between imagining himself a hunter and actually killing a living creature. Once he begins to kill and gets over his initial squeamishness, he will become ruthless.

3. Ralph says of Simon, "He's queer. He's funny." What kind of a boy is Simon?

> Simon is one of Ralph's most loyal and helpful workers. Yet, when he has some free time, he goes off by himself to find a place to be quiet and to think. Society, like the boys, distrusts those who are loners. The love of beauty and solitude is suspect.

4. After Maurice and Roger destroy the littluns' sand castles, Roger stalks the young boy named Henry. When he begins to throw stones, why does he just throw them near him instead of directly at him?

> The old laws of church and school and family still hold him back.

5. What causes the hunters, who had promised to keep the fire burning, to neglect it and allow it to go out?

> Jack's immediate goal is to kill a pig; this is all he can think about. The building of a fire and the rescue are long-term goals. Savages cannot deal with long-term goals; they only live in the present, for instant gratification of their immediate needs.

6. Why does Jack paint his face?

> Jack's clay paint effectively blots out his real features, and he can become an anonymous savage.

16

Chapters 5 - 6

1. How does the author show us that Ralph is finally beginning to face the realities of their existence?

   The author tells us that Ralph does not really like to live a life where he has to watch where he walks; nor does he like filthy, frayed clothing or dirty, tangled, long hair. To Ralph, this adventure is becoming messy and real and scary.

2. Compare Ralph's treatment of the littluns with Jack's.

   Ralph tries to calm their fears and give them a sense of security. Jack intimidates them and frightens them.

3. What is Simon saying when he thinks the "beast" may be inside they boys themselves?

   He is trying to say that the dark side of the human personality can destroy mankind. Reason and imagination are the only checks men have to quell this "dark side."

4. What do Sam and Eric tell the boys they have seen? What is it actually?

   They tell the boys that they have seen a beast. It was actually the corpse of a parachutist.

5. Why do Ralph and Jack decide to go find the beast?

   They know that they must face the beast if they are to have any hopes of being free from their fears on the island.

Chapters 7 - 8

1. How does Ralph react when a boar comes charging down the path?

   Ralph throws his wooden spear and scores a lucky hit. It does not deter the boar, but it does show Ralph a side of himself that he has refused to acknowledge. He exults in his ability to wound a living creature.

2. To what does Ralph's demonstration of his hunting prowess lead?

   Robert pretended to be an animal and snarled at Ralph. The boys got into a hunting frenzy, at first jokingly and then really jabbing and poking at Robert. They went out of control.

3. What did the boys see on the mountaintop?

   At first they saw a lump or a hump where no rock should be. Then, conquering his nausea, Ralph stood up and saw "something like a great ape." The wind blew and the billowing parachute lifted the head and torso of the "ape," showing them "the ruin of a face."

4. Why is the action of the story increasingly taking place in the near darkness or in the deep night when only the moon and stars give a little light?

   Darkness has always symbolized something evil as light has symbolized the "good." "The Prince of Darkness" is another name for the devil, evil.

5. How does Ralph's waning confidence in himself show in his words and actions?

He has begun to bite his nails. He shudders involuntarily and twists his hands unconsciously. He has become bitter at the collapse of his dreams and plans. When Piggy asks, "What are we going to do?," for the first time Ralph answers, "I don't know."

6. Although he is not able to get the boys to vote Ralph out of office as chief, Jack manages to overthrow Ralph's authority anyway. How?

He simply announces, "I'm not going to play anymore. Not with you." His statements reflect the notion that the predicament of the boys is an adventure, a game. With a typical child's reaction, he decides not to "play" anymore since he doesn't like the rules of Ralph's game. He goes off to "play" by himself, to get some of the kids to "play" <u>his</u> game.

7. Jack suggests a way to keep the beast happy. What is it?

He suggests that they should give the beast part of each kill they make.

8. Describe Simon's strange encounter with the Lord of the Flies.

Whether Simon's encounter is imagined, dreamed, or supernatural is not very clear. The content of the Lord's message, though, is central to the book. The Lord of the Flies explains to Simon that it is useless to try to kill the beast. "I am a part of you," he says. Golding seems to imply that no matter what name you give to evil, be it sin, the devil, neurosis, hate, violence, terrorism, or sheer wanton destruction, these traits are inside of man. The conflict between good and evil is inside each boy on the island as it is inside all of us. This book, which pictures the downfall of a small society on an unknown island, also gives a portrait of what it means to be human.

9. Who or what is the Lord of the Flies?

The Lord of the Flies, represented by the pig's head, is evil.

Chapters 9 - 11

1. What does Simon find when he finally reaches the Beast?

He discovers the truth that the beast is actually a dead pilot. The lines of his parachute have been tangled in such a way that when the wind blows and inflates the chute, it lifts the dead figure into a sitting position and thereby gives the figure a semblance of life.

2. What happens to Simon when he returns to the group?

The hunters, doing their ritual dance, kill him. He is never able to deliver a coherent message to them. He stumbles off of the cliff and falls to the sands below.

3. As a result of the storm with its high winds and high tides, what happens to the bodies of Simon and the parachutist?

They are taken out to sea.

4. What does Jack plan to steal from Ralph and Piggy?
   He plans to steal fire from them.

5. What will Jack do if someone interferes with him?
   He says, "we will do our dance again," meaning the hunters will kill the one who interferes.

6. What happens to the conch and to Piggy?
   Roger releases the huge boulder and it shatters the conch which Piggy had been holding. It also shatters Piggy, who falls forty feet, landing on his back on a flat rock, somewhat like the ancient sacrificial victims were placed on an altar and offered up to some savage god.

7. What are Jack's plans for Ralph?
   He plans to hunt him down and kill him.

8. What course of action does Ralph take?
   Ralph has to either fight or flee. Not being able to defeat all of the hunters, he flees.

Chapter 12
1. What is Ralph's reaction when he encounters the pig's skull?
   "A sick fear and rage swept through him." He hits the skull with his fist and splits it open; it lies on the ground, still grinning at him.

2. Driven by fear and hunger, Ralph manages to make contact with Samneric who are standing guard at Castle Rock. Of what do they warn him?
   They warn him that the hunters are going to hunt him down tomorrow, and they tell him that Roger has sharpened a stick at both ends.

3. In what ways does the tribe try to hunt down Ralph?
   They roll boulders down the hill to try to hit him or cause him to run. Then they try to smoke him out. When he goes to the forest, they continue to try to track him down like a pig.

4. What or who saves Ralph in the end?
   His savior is a British naval officer who represents the adult, civilized world, a world combining the military (hunters) and civilians (civilization).

19

MULTIPLE CHOICE STUDY GUIDE/QUIZ QUESTIONS - *Lord of the Flies*

<u>Chapters 1-2</u>

1. Character Identification - Match each character with the correct description.

1. Ralph	a. choir leader, "silly without ugliness"
2. Piggy	b. handsome, athletic, natural leader
3. Simon	c. Sam's brother
4. Jack	d. "grinning all the time," choir boy
5. Sam	e. intelligent, not very active
6. Maurice	f. numerous small children of the group
7. Roger	g. one of the pair of identical twins
8. Littluns	h. poetic, sensitive loner
9. Eric	i. "slight, furtive," natural tendency to cruelty

2. How did the boys happen to come to the island?
   A. They were on a Scout camping trip.
   B. They were shipwrecked during a sailboat race.
   C. They were ejected from a flaming airplane.
   D. They had stolen a boat and were running away from school.

3. What do the boys have that is the symbol of authority in the society they form?
   A. A conch shell
   B. A British flag
   C. A Bible
   D. A whale jaw bone

4. What does the reader learn about Jack when he slashed the green candle buds?
   A. He is optimistic about their chances for survival.
   B. He is afraid of snakes.
   C. He is creative in his thinking.
   D. His method of dealing with the world is violent.

5. What does Jack's hesitation to kill the piglet show?
   A. He gets sick at the sight of blood.
   B. He must learn to put aside his inhibitions.
   C. He has never used a knife before.
   D. He is secretly a coward.

6. Who are the hunters, and what is their job?
    A. The littluns; looking for ships and planes
    B. Samneric; killing dangerous animals
    C. The choirboys; getting food
    D. Simon, Piggy, Ralph; governing the boys

7. What does a Little 'Un think he has seen in the forest?
    A. A snake-thing which he calls a beastie
    B. Adults' footprints
    C. A pack of wild dogs
    D. The skeleton of a large animal

8. How and why do the boys make fire?
    A. They do it for protection from wild animals. One boy had a pack of
       matches which they use.
    B. The fire was started by lightening. The boys kept it burning.
    C. The Little "Uns were afraid of the dark. One of the older boys found some
       fuel that had leaked from the crashed plane, and carried it to the site in
       a shell.
    D. It was a rescue signal. They use Piggy's glasses as a "burning glass."

9. Why does the boy's plan for rescue fail?
    A. The ground and wood were wet and the fire would not burn.
    B. They didn't have a well-thought out plan to control the fire.
    C. It was foggy and no one could see the signal.
    D. They were afraid to get close enough to keep the fire going.

<u>Chapters 3-4</u>

10. Although Ralph criticizes the boys for their lack of cooperation, does he bear some of the responsibility for the failures of the group to achieve its goals?
    A. Ralph is partially responsible. He has the desire to bring civilization, but lacks the competence to do so. He believes life is too much like a story.
    B. Ralph is not responsible at all. He has done all he could to get the boys to cooperate, and they have chosen not to.
    C. Ralph bears a large part of the responsibility. He is not using his leadership abilities in a way that is in the best interests of the whole group
    D. Ralph bears only a very small part of the responsibility. He is really much to shy and fearful to be able to organize the boys.

11. How has Jack's personality developed during his stay on the island?
    A. Jack is developing into a mystic and poet.
    B. Jack is becoming withdrawn and fearful.
    C. Jack is degenerating from a civilized boy to a primitive, near animal level.
    D. Jack is emerging as a clear-headed, well-organized thinker, and a natural leader.

12. Ralph says of Simon, "He's queer. He's funny." What kind of a boy is Simon?
    A. Simon is a natural comic. He keeps the group's spirits up with his unfailing sense of humor.
    B. Simon is a loyal and helpful worker. He likes to be alone to think and feel the beauty of the forest.
    C. Simon is becoming more and more violent. He is losing his sense of civilization.
    D. Simon is fearful and belligerent. The other boys don't want to be around him.

13. After Maurice and Roger destroy the littluns' sand castles, Roger stalks the young boy named Henry. When he begins to throw stones, why does Roger just throw near Henry instead of directly at him?
    A. Roger is scared off by a noise in the jungle behind him.
    B. Roger is afraid that the littluns will hit back.
    C. Maurice tells Roger he (Maurice) will beat him up if he hits any of the littluns.
    D. The old laws of school, church, and family still hold him back.

14. What causes the hunters, who had promised to keep the fire burning, to neglect it and allow it to go out?
    A. They become more interested in trying to build a canoe.
    B. They are becoming more savage, and can only think about hunting.
    C. They think that the other boys will get over their fear of the dark better if there is no light at all for a few nights.
    D. They are inexperienced and don't really know how to keep it burning.

15. Why does Jack paint his face?
    A. The paint protects his sensitive skin from the sun.
    B. He thinks it will cheer up the others.
    C. He uses the paint as a mask to blot out his real self and become a savage.
    D. He tries to scare the littluns into obeying him.

Chapters 5-6

16. How does the author show us that Ralph is finally beginning to face the realities of their existence?
   A. Ralph has begun to tell the others that they will never be rescued.
   B. Ralph begins having nightmares and crying out in his sleep.
   C. Ralph increases his efforts to have the boys build a canoe.
   D. Ralph becomes distressed at his filthy clothes and dirty long hair.

17. Compare Ralph's treatment of the littluns with Jack's.
   A. Ralph tries to calm their fears and give them a sense of security. Jack intimidates and frightens them.
   B. Ralph treats them harshly, thinking it is for their own good. Jack protects them and makes sure they have enough to eat.
   C. Ralph is kind and understanding. Jack fears the littluns will like Ralph better, so he tries to win them by being kinder than Ralph, although it is a false kindness.
   D. Neither Ralph nor Jack have much experience with younger children. They soon tire of the littluns' immaturity and ignore them.

18. What is Simon saying when he thinks the "beast" may be inside the boys themselves?
   A. They have eaten some poisoned meat.
   B. None of them are really human.
   C. The dark side of the human personality can destroy mankind.
   D. It is all in their imaginations.

19. What do Sam and Eric tell the others they have seen? What is it actually?
   A. They say they have seen a ship. It is really a school of dolphins.
   B. They say they have seen a beast. It is really the corpse of a parachutist.
   C. They say they have seen another signal fire. It is really bombs exploding in the distance.
   D. They say they have seen a witch doctor. It is really Jack, trying to scare them.

20. Why do Ralph and Jack decide to go find the beast?
   A. They want to prove that they are really good friends.
   B. They know killing it will provide food for a long time.
   C. They think the others are silly and want to show that there is no beast.
   D. They know they must face the beast if they are to have any hopes of being free from their fears.

Chapters 7-8
21. How does Ralph react when a boar comes charging down the path?
    A. His spear hits, but does not deter, the boar. His excitement at wounding a living creature shows Ralph his dark side.
    B. Ralph is afraid to throw his spear. He is able to hide from the boar, but realizes how fearful he really is.
    C. Ralph refuses to hurt the animal. He is proud of his ability to retain some semblance of civilization.
    D. Ralph injures the boar. He does not feel good about his actions, but rationalizes them in the name of self-defense.

22. To what does Ralph's demonstration of his hunting prowess lead?
    A. It re-establishes him as the leader, and the boys rekindle the signal fire.
    B. It makes the littluns afraid of him and they run and hide.
    C. Jack realizes Ralph's strength and vows to fight him.
    D. The boys go into a hunting frenzy and begin jabbing and poking at Robert.

23. What did the boys see on the mountaintop?
    A. They see a strange, ape-like beast that seems to move back and forth.
    B. They see a light on the water in the distance.
    C. They see the remains of an ancient burial ground.
    D. They see a pack of wild dogs eating a piglet.

24. How does the author show the increase in evil in the boys?
    A. He describes storm clouds overhead and rough seas.
    B. More of the action takes place in the dark or deep night.
    C. The boys start telling each other scary stories about ghosts and devils.
    D. Jack and the hunters find animal bones that they sharpen and wear that symbolize evil.

25. How does Ralph's waning confidence in himself show in his words and actions?
    A. He laughs hysterically whenever one of the boys asks him a question.
    B. He complains of shortness of breath and chest pains.
    C. He begins sleeping most of the time, waking only to eat.
    D. He starts biting his nails, shuddering involuntarily, and twisting his hands.

26. How does Jack overthrow Ralph's authority?
    A. Jack gets the boys to vote Ralph out of office.
    B. Jack tells the others he is the oldest, and the oldest should rule.
    C. Jack announces he won't play anymore, and goes off by himself.
    D. Jack challenges Ralph to a spear-throwing contest and wins.

27. Jack suggests a way to keep the beast happy. What is it?
    A. Make a special house for the beast.
    B. Give the beast part of each kill.
    C. Sing to the beast every night.
    D. Leave the beast alone and move to the other side of the island.

28. What is the meaning of the Lord of the Flies' message to Simon?
    A. Evil is a trait inside of man.
    B. Dreams can be more powerful than reality.
    C. It is unhealthy to eat uncooked meat.
    D. If they ignore the beast it will go away.

29. Who or what is the Lord of the Flies?
    A. It is the name they have given the dead pilot.
    B. It is a large, poisonous insect that thrives on the island.
    C. It is a game the littluns play to pass the time.
    D. It is the sow's head, and represents evil.

Chapters 9-11

30. What does Simon find when he finally reaches the beast?
    A. It is a dead pilot. The parachute is tangled and inflates when the wind blows.
    B. It is a statue, probably carved by a tribe who once lived on the island.
    C. It really is a wild beast. He runs in fear.
    D. It is a pile of rocks and branches that Jack made to scare the others.

31. What happens to Simon when he returns to the group?
    A. He keeps quiet because he knows they won't believe him.
    B. He joins in the dance and becomes evil himself.
    C. He tells Ralph the truth, and then goes off to live alone.
    D. The hunters kill him before he can tell them anything.

32. What happens to the bodies of Simon and the Parachutist?
    A. The boys use them to rekindle the fire.
    B. They are eaten by the wild boars.
    C. Ralph and Piggy feel guilty and bury them.
    D. They are taken out to sea by the high winds and tides.

33. What does Jack plan to steal from Ralph and Piggy?
    A. The only blanket
    B. The fruit they have collected
    C. The fire
    D. Their spears

34. What will Jack do if someone interferes with him?
    A. He will put them in the small jail cell he has built of stone and branches.
    B. He will drive them away from the group and force them to live alone.
    C. He will order the hunters to kill them.
    D. He will break one of their legs.

35. What happens to the conch and Piggy?
    A. Piggy steals the conch and escapes into the jungle.
    B. They are both eaten by a wild boar.
    C. Piggy saves the conch but loses his glasses.
    D. They are both shattered by the huge boulder.

36. What are Jack's plans for Ralph?
    A. Jack will drive Ralph off into the jungle.
    B. Jack will hunt for and kill Ralph.
    C. Jack will let Ralph join the hunters if he gives up his leadership role.
    D. Jack realizes he is wrong and tries to become friends again.

37. What course of action does Ralph take? Why?
    A. He runs away because he cannot fight all of the hunters.
    B. He cries and begs Jack not to hurt him.
    C. He attacks Jack with a spear.
    D. He agrees to join Jack and the hunters.

Chapter 12
38. What is Ralph's reaction when he encounters the pig's skull?
    A. He throws it and it shatters on the rocks.
    B. He hits it with his fist and splits it open.
    C. He buries it so the others won't find it.
    D. He keeps it to use to scare the others.

39. What do Samneric tell Ralph?
    A. Roger has sharpened a stick at both ends and the hunters will go after him the next day.
    B. Jack has promised to kill any boy who gives Ralph food.
    C. The hunters are ready to overthrow Jack and reinstate Ralph.
    D. They know of a cave where Ralph can hide.

40. Which is not one of the ways the hunters used to find Ralph?
    A. Smoke him out
    B. Roll boulders down the hill
    C. Make nets of jungle vines
    D. Track him like a pig

41. How is Ralph saved in the end?
    A. The littluns push Jack off the mountain top into the sea.
    B. He is stronger than Jack and defeats him.
    C. He swims to the safety of another island.
    D. A British naval officer finds him.

ANSWER KEY - MULTIPLE CHOICE STUDY/QUIZ QUESTIONS
Lord of the Flies

1.
1. Ralph, B.
2. Piggy, E.
3. Simon, H.
4. Jack, A.
5. Sam, G.
6. Maurice, D.
7. Roger, I.
8. Littluns, F.
9. Eric, C.

2. C
3. A
4. D
5. B
6. C
7. A
8. D
9. B
10. A
11. C
12. B
13. D
14. B
15. C
16. D
17. A

18. C
19. B
20. C
21. A
22. D
23. A
24. B
25. D
26. C
27. B
28. A
29. D
30. A
31. D
32. D
33. C
34. C
35. D
36. B
37. A
38. B
39. A
40. C
41. D

PREREADING VOCABULARY WORKSHEETS

VOCABULARY - *Lord of the Flies*

<u>Chapters 1-2</u>, Part I: Using Prior Knowledge and Contextual Clues
     Below are the sentences in which the vocabulary words appear in the text. Read the sentences. Use any clues you can find in the sentence combined with your prior knowledge, and write what you think the underlined words mean in the space provided.

1. Ralph had been deceived before now by the <u>specious</u> appearance of depth in a beach pool and he approached this one preparing to be disappointed.

2. The most usual feature of the rock was a pink cliff surmounted by a <u>skewed</u> block.

3. There was another island: a rock, almost detached, standing like a fort, facing them across the green with one bold, pink <u>bastion</u>.

4. There came a pause, a <u>hiatus</u>, the pig continued to scream and the creepers to jerk, and the blade continued to flash at the end of a bony arm.

5. He <u>gesticulated</u> widely.

6. Then, with the martyred expression of a parent who has to keep up with the senseless <u>ebullience</u> of the children...

7. A <u>pall</u> stretched for miles away from the island.

Part II: Determining the Meaning

___ 1. specious	A. a break
___ 2. skewed	B. a well-fortified position
___ 3. bastion	C. a gloomy effect
___ 4. hiatus	D. plausible but actually false
___ 5. gesticulated	E. zestful enthusiasm
___ 6. ebullience	F. turned to one side
___ 7. pall	G. made hand motions

Vocabulary - *Lord of the Flies*

<u>Chapters 3-4</u> Part I: Using Prior Knowledge and Contextual Clues
 Use any clues you can find in the sentence combined with your prior knowledge, and write what you think the underlined words mean in the space provided.

8. The tree trunks and the creepers that <u>festooned</u> them lost themselves in a green dusk thirty feet above him . . .

9. Jack lifted his head and stared at the <u>inscrutable</u> masses of creeper that lay across the trail.

10. The <u>opaque</u>, mad look came into his eyes again.

11. But Jack was pointing to the high <u>declivities</u> that led down from the mountain to the flatter part of the island.

12. With <u>impalpable</u> organs of sense they examined this new field.

13. Beside the pool his <u>sinewy</u> body held up a mask that drew their eyes and appalled them.

14. There had grown up <u>tacitly</u> among the biguns the opinion that Piggy was an outsider, not only by accent, which did not matter, but by fat...

Part II: Determining the Meaning
 You have tried to figure out the meanings of the vocabulary words. Now match the vocabulary words to their dictionary definitions. If there are words for which you cannot figure out the definition by contextual clues and by process of elimination, look them up in a dictionary.

___ 8. festooned	A. without being spoken
___ 9. inscrutable	B. downward slopes
___ 10. opaque	C. decorated
___ 11. declivities	D. lean and muscular
___ 12. impalpable	E. light can't get through it
___ 13. sinewy	F. impenetrable
___ 14. tacitly	G. intangible; not perceived by touch

Vocabulary - *Lord of the Flies*

Chapters 5-6 Part I: Using Prior Knowledge and Contextual Clues
   Use any clues you can find in the sentence combined with your prior knowledge, and write what you think the underlined words mean in the space provided.

15. He found himself understanding the wearisomeness of this life, where every patch was an improvisation and a considerable part of one's waking life was spent watching one's feet.

16. Then, at the apex, the grass was thick again because no one sat there.

17. The derisive laughter that rose had fear in it and condemnation.

18. At first he was a silent effigy of sorrow; but then the lamentation rose out of him, loud and sustained as the conch.

19. A shadow fronted him tempestuously.

20. . . . lying in the long grass, was he was living through circumstances in which the incantation of his address was powerless to help him.

21. Simon, walking in front of Ralph, felt a flicker of incredulity-a beast with claws that scratch

22. The taut blue horizon encircled them, broken only by the mountain-top.

Part II: Determining the Meaning: Match the vocabulary words to their dictionary definitions.

___ 15. improvisation	A. scornful
___ 16. apex	B. tight
___ 17. derisive	C. the highest point
___ 18. effigy	D. disbelief
___ 19. tempestuously	E. a likeness or image
___ 20. incantation	F. to invent without preparation
___ 21. incredulity	G. like a storm; turbulently
___ 22. taut	H. a verbal charm or spell

Vocabulary - *Lord of the Flies*

<u>Chapters 7-8</u> Part I: Using Prior Knowledge and Contextual Clues
   Use any clues you can find in the sentence combined with your prior knowledge, and write what you think the underlined words mean in the space provided.

23. . . . if you could forget how dun and unvisited were the ferny <u>coverts</u> on either side, then there was a chance that you might put the beast out of your mind for a while.

24. On the other side of the island, swathed at midday with mirage, defended by the shield of the quiet lagoon, one might dream of rescue; but here, faced by the brute <u>obtuseness</u> of the ocean, the miles of division...

25. For most of the way they were forced right down to the bare rock by the water and had to edge along between that and the dark <u>luxuriance</u> of the forest.

26. So they sat, the rocking, tapping <u>impervious</u> Roger and Ralph, fuming.

27. Piggy gave up the attempt to <u>rebuke</u> Ralph.

28. The wood he fetched was close at hand, a fallen tree on the platform that they did not need for the assembly, yet to the others the <u>sanctity</u> of the platform had protected even what was useless there.

29. A little apart from the rest, sunk in deep <u>maternal</u> bliss, lay the largest sow of the lot.

30. The half-shut eyes were dim with the infinite <u>cynicism</u> of adult life.

Part II: Determining the Meaning: Match the vocabulary words to their dictionary definitions.

___ 23. coverts   A. having rich or profuse growth
___ 24. obtuseness   B. relating to motherhood
___ 25. luxuriance   C. thick underbrush providing cover
___ 26. impervious   D. attitude scornful of the motives or virtues of others
___ 27. rebuke   E. dullness; flatness; lack of sharp edges
___ 28. sanctity   F. to criticize or reprimand
___ 29. maternal   G. incapable of being affected
___ 30. cynicism   H. sacredness; godliness

Vocabulary - *Lord of the Flies*

<u>Chapters 9-11</u> Part I: Using Prior Knowledge and Contextual Clues
    Use any clues you can find in the sentence combined with your prior knowledge, and write what you think the underlined words mean in the space provided.

31. Piggy once more was the center of social <u>derision</u> so that everyone felt cheerful and normal.

32. He ceased to work at his tooth and sat still, <u>assimilating</u> the possibilities of irresponsible authority.

33. The night was cool and <u>purged</u> of immediate terror.

34. The twins watched anxiously and Piggy sat expressionless behind the luminous wall of his <u>myopia</u>.

35. Piggy nodded <u>propitiatingly</u>. "You're chief, Ralph. You remember everything."

36. High above them from the <u>pinnacles</u> came a sudden shout and then an imitation war-cry that was answered by a dozen voices from behind the rock.

37. <u>Truculently</u> they squared up to each other but kept just out of fighting distance.

Part II: Determining the Meaning: Match the vocabulary words to their dictionary definitions.

___ 31. derision
___ 32. assimilating
___ 33. purged
___ 34. myopia
___ 35. propitatingly
___ 36. pinnacles
___ 37. truculently

A. absorbing
B. tall, pointed formations
C. disposed to fight
D. scorn or ridicule
E. a visual defect like nearsightedness
F. freed from impurities
G. appeasingly; trying to please

Vocabulary - *Lord of the Flies*

<u>Chapter 12</u> Part I: Using Prior Knowledge and Contextual Clues
Use any clues you can find in the sentence combined with your prior knowledge, and write what you think the underlined words mean in the space provided.

38. A star appeared behind them and was momentarily <u>eclipsed</u> by some movement.

39. To carry he must speak louder; and this would rouse those striped and <u>inimical</u> creatures from their feasting by the fire.

40. Then the red thing was past and the <u>elephantine</u> progress diminished toward the sea.

41. He heard a curious trickling sound and then a louder <u>crepitation</u> as if someone were unwrapping great sheets of cellophane.

42. . . . a somber noise across which the ululations were scribbled <u>excruciatingly</u> as on slate.

43. For a moment he had a fleeting picture of the strange <u>glamour</u> that had once invested the beaches.

Part II: Determining the Meaning: Match the vocabulary words to their dictionary definitions.

___ 38. eclipsed
___ 39. inimical
___ 40. elephantine
___ 41. crepitation
___ 42. excruciatingly
___ 43. glamour

A. crackling sound
B. ponderously clumsy
C. magic spell; enchantment
D. unfriendly; hostile
E. obscured; blocked from view
F. intensely; painfully

ANSWER KEY - VOCABULARY
Lord of the Flies

1. D	23. C
2. F	24. E
3. B	25. A
4. A	26. G
5. G	27. F
6. E	28. H
7. C	29. B
	30. D
8. C	31. D
9. F	32. A
10. E	33. F
11. B	34. E
12. G	35. G
13. D	36. B
14. A	37. C
15. F	38. E
16. C	39. D
17. A	40. B
18. E	41. A
19. G	42. F
20. H	43. C
21. D	
22. B	

DAILY LESSONS

LESSONS ONE AND TWO

Objectives
      1. To introduce the *Lord of the Flies* unit.
      2. To distribute books and other related materials

NOTES: It really helps students get in the mood for this story and this activity if your room is turned into a tropical island as much as possible. Check with your public library to see if they have any soundtracks, videos or other recordings of tropical birds, waterfalls, etc. and use the soundtrack as background sounds. If you can't find a soundtrack, perhaps your local pet store would lend you a couple of canaries. Also, perhaps some of your local florists or greenhouses would donate or loan you some hanging plants or small trees for your room. You might also check with your local carpet discounters to see if they have a remnant of green indoor-outdoor carpeting for your floor. Anything that has been donated to your project from your local retailers could be used a prizes for the best writing assignments, etc.

Activity #1

      If possible, push all the students' desks back against one wall. As students come in to your class, keep the lights off and have your tropical sound effects playing. A few natural logs to sit on is a nice touch. Otherwise, students can just sit on the floor.

      Tell students that it is early in the morning and their airplane has just crashed on a deserted island. The pilot is dead. They are the only people on the island. Now they, as a group, have to decide what to do to survive.

      Give students ample time to role-play this scenario. Some students may need more structure than this open-ended assignment. If your students do, put a checklist on the bulletinboard of things they need to accomplish. If your students can handle the open-ended assignment but need motivation, you may want to tell students that each person will be graded on his/her participation in this activity.

      You can make this assignment as real-to-life as you wish. Students who are responsible for creating shelter, for example, could actually have to produce a shelter in your classroom. Students who are responsible for providing food could actually have to bring food into class during this unit. Students who are responsible for gathering wood, creating clothing, creating tools, dishes, etc. could also all have to actually produce their respective assignments. The leaders and the students themselves should determine by when all of these goods will be necessary (due dates for the assignments).

      This unit allows one and a half class periods of class time for students to "get into" this activity, to begin making plans and assignments. Adjust the time as needed for your class.

Note also that during this unit, the role-playing continues with Writing Assignment 1. Students are to maintain a daily journal, a log of what happens in their island lives each day. Some time is allowed at the beginning of each class period for students to work on their journal entries. You can either make this an individual or a group writing assignment. This unit treats it as an individual assignment so that each student may use his/her own imagination and create his/her own story. At the end of the unit, then, students share their journal stories with the whole class.

Activity #2
    Distribute the materials students will use in this unit. Explain in detail how students are to use these materials.

    Study Guides Students should read the study guide questions for each reading assignment prior to beginning the reading assignment to get a feeling for what events and ideas are important in the section they are about to read. After reading the section, students will (as a class or individually) answer the questions to review the important events and ideas from that section of the book. Students should keep the study guides as study materials for the unit test.

    Vocabulary Prior to reading a reading assignment, students will do vocabulary work related to the section of the book they are about to read. Following the completion of the reading of the book, there will be a vocabulary review of all the words used in the vocabulary assignments. Students should keep their vocabulary work as study materials for the unit test.

    Reading Assignment Sheet You need to fill in the reading assignment sheet to let students know by when their reading has to be completed. You can either write the assignment sheet up on a side blackboard or bulletinboard and leave it there for students to see each day, or you can "ditto" copies for each student to have. In either case, you should advise students to become very familiar with the reading assignments so they know what is expected of them.

    Extra Activities Center The Extra Activities portion of this unit contains suggestions for an extra library of related books and articles in your classroom as well as crossword and word search puzzles. Make an extra activities center in your room where you will keep these materials for students to use. (Bring the books and articles in from the library and keep several copies of the puzzles on hand.) Explain to students that these materials are available for students to use when they finish reading assignments or other class work early.

    Nonfiction Assignment Sheet Explain to students that they each are to read at least one non-fiction piece at some time during the unit. Students will fill out a nonfiction assignment sheet after completing the reading to help you evaluate their reading experiences and to help the students think about and evaluate their own reading experiences.

    <u>Books</u> Each school has its own rules and regulations regarding student use of school books. Advise students of the procedures that are normal for your school.

    <u>Writing Assignment #1</u> Distribute the journal writing assignment and discuss the directions in detail.

Activity #3

    Preview the study questions and have students do the vocabulary work for Chapters 1-2 of *Lord of the Flies*. If students do not finish this assignment during this class period, they should complete it prior to the next class meeting.

NONFICTION ASSIGNMENT SHEET
(To be completed after reading the required nonfiction article)

Name _____ Date _____

Title of Nonfiction Read _____

Written By _____ Publication Date _____

I. Factual Summary: Write a short summary of the piece you read.

II. Vocabulary
    1. With which vocabulary words in the piece did you encounter some degree of difficulty?

    2. How did you resolve your lack of understanding with these words?

III. Interpretation: What was the main point the author wanted you to get from reading his work?

IV. Criticism
    1. With which points of the piece did you agree or find easy to accept? Why?

    2. With which points of the piece did you disagree or find difficult to believe? Why?

V. Personal Response: What do you think about this piece? <u>OR</u> How does this piece influence your ideas?

WRITING ASSIGNMENT #1 - *Lord of the Flies*

PROMPT

You and your classmates have been stranded on this deserted island. You have begun to make plans for your survival. During the next couple of weeks you will be off on an adventure of a lifetime, struggling for your very survival in a tropical paradise.

Fortunately, even though the plane crashed, you have managed to find a notebook of blank paper and some pencils. You, then, have been put in charge of maintaining a daily log--a record of the things that happen to you and your classmates while you are on this island.

Each day you are required to write down the events of the day before. Each entry must be at least about 1/2 notebook page long. Certainly, on some days you will have more to report than on others. Overall, though, it is your responsibility to maintain a thorough, detailed account of your adventures on this island. (Have you and your classmates named this island yet?)

PREWRITING

Your prewriting stage for this assignment is going to be an on-going thing. That is, your entries have to have a certain continuity. If someone falls and breaks a leg one day, that person cannot be mountain climbing the next day as if nothing had happened, for example. The prewriting stage can't just be done in class; think about it in your spare time. What kinds of adventures could/would you and your classmates have? Keep in mind that different people have different personalities more suited to some activities than others. Most of all, let your imagination soar. Conflicts are bound to arise. Problems will happen. Good times will be had. Create your own story of adventure, danger, romance and intrigue. As you think of ideas for your story, jot them down no matter where you are, so you will remember them when you are ready to write. By the time you are several days into this assignment, you should have a little stack of notes to help guide you.

DRAFTING

Think of your log as a kind of diary, if that helps you get started. Write down the events that happened. Feel free to inject your own comments and observations. A little humor never hurts. Look at the notes you have made for ideas. Most importantly, put pen to paper and start. Start first with what happened yesterday. Give a little background about who was on the plane and where you were going. Describe the crash and the events that followed. Then, just keep your imagination flowing and start creating your island world.

PROOFREADING

Take time to proofread each entry for grammatical or spelling errors. Try to make your entries neat so that when your journal is found a hundred years from now, or if you are rescued and you decide to publish your book and make a fortune, someone else will easily be able to read your journal entries.

LESSON THREE

<u>Objectives</u>
   1. To give students time to work on their journal entries
   2. To read chapters 1-2
   3. To give students practice reading orally
   4. To evaluate students' oral reading

<u>NOTE:</u> If your students are going "whole hog" on this unit and doing it as realistically as possible, you will need to allow additional class time for planning, eating, building, etc. You'll just have to use your own best judgement as to how much time to allow.

<u>Activity #1</u>
   Give students ten minutes or so to work on their journal entries.

<u>Activity #2</u>
   Have students read chapters 1-2 of *Lord of the Flies* out loud in class. You probably know the best way to get readers with your class; pick students at random, ask for volunteers, or use whatever method works best for your group. If you have not yet completed an oral reading evaluation for your students this marking period, this would be a good opportunity to do so. A form is included with this unit for your convenience.

   If students do not complete reading chapters 1-2 in class, they should do so prior to your next class meeting.

ORAL READING EVALUATION - *Lord of the Flies*

Name _____ Class_____ Date _____

SKILL	EXCELLENT	GOOD	AVERAGE	FAIR	POOR
Fluency	5	4	3	2	1
Clarity	5	4	3	2	1
Audibility	5	4	3	2	1
Pronunciation	5	4	3	2	1
_____	5	4	3	2	1
_____	5	4	3	2	1

Total _____   Grade _____

Comments:

LESSON FOUR

Objectives
1. To give students time to work on their journal entries
2. To review the main ideas and events from chapters 1-2
3. To do the prereading work for chapters 3-4
4. To read chapters 3-4
5. To complete the oral reading evaluations

Activity #1

Give students ten minutes or so to work on their journal entries.

Activity #2

Give students a few minutes to formulate answers for the study guide questions for chapters 1-2, and then discuss the answers to the questions in detail. Write the answers on the board or overhead transparency so students can have the correct answers for study purposes. Note: It is a good practice in public speaking and leadership skills for individual students to take charge of leading the discussions of the study questions. Perhaps a different student could go to the front of the class and lead the discussion each day that the study questions are discussed during this unit. Of course, the teacher should guide the discussion when appropriate and be sure to fill in any gaps the students leave.

Activity #3

Give students ten to fifteen minutes to look over the study questions and do the vocabulary work for chapters 3-4.

Activity #4

Have students read chapters 3-4 orally in class. Complete the oral reading evaluations. If students do not finish reading this section in class, they should do so prior to the next class period.

LESSON FIVE

Objectives
     1. To give students time to work on their journal entries
     2. To review the main ideas and events from chapters 3-4
     3. To do the prereading work for chapters 5-6
     4. To read chapters 5-6

Activity #1
     Give students ten minutes or so to work on their journal entries.

Activity #2
     Give students a few minutes to formulate answers for the study guide questions for chapters 3-4, and then discuss the answers to the questions in detail. Write the answers on the board or overhead transparency so students can have the correct answers for study purposes.

Activity #3
     Give students ten to fifteen minutes to look over the study questions and do the vocabulary work for chapters 5-6.

Activity #4
     Have students read chapters 5-6 silently in class. If students do not finish reading this section in class, they should do so prior to the next class period.

LESSON SIX

Objectives
    1. To give students the opportunity to explore nonfiction topics related to the story
    2. To give students the opportunity to use the library
    3. To broaden students' knowledge of our world
    4. To give students time to work on their journal entries

Activity #1
    Take students to the library. Explain to them that this is their opportunity to complete the nonfiction reading assignment which accompanies this unit. Students are to find nonfiction books or articles in some way relating to *Lord of the Flies*. Students are to use this time to find nonfiction materials that interest them and to begin reading. Remind students to complete the Nonfiction Assignment Sheet after they have done their reading.

Remind students that they will be giving a little oral report about their nonfiction reading in Lesson Fourteen. (Give students a day and a date.)

    Suggested Topics (Feel free to add to this list.)

    Survival skills
    Camping
    History of civilization
    Social psychology
    Articles of criticism about *Lord of the Flies*
    Airplane crashes and survivors
    Hunting

Activity #2
    If students finish the nonfiction assignment early, they should use the leftover class time to work on their journal entries.

LESSON SEVEN

Objectives

    1. To give students time to work on their journal entries
    2. To review the main ideas and events from chapters 5-6
    3. To do the prereading work for chapters 7-8
    4. To read chapters 7-8

Activity #1

Give students ten minutes or so to work on their journal entries.

Activity #2

Give students a few minutes to formulate answers for the study guide questions for chapters 5-6, and then discuss the answers to the questions in detail. Write the answers on the board or overhead transparency.

Activity #3

Give students ten to fifteen minutes to look over the study questions and do the vocabulary work for chapters 7-8.

Activity #4

Have students read chapters 7-8 silently in class. If students do not finish reading this section in class, they should do so prior to the next class period.

LESSON EIGHT

Objectives
      1. To give students time to work on their journal entries
      2. To review the main ideas and events from chapters 7-8
      3. To do the prereading work for chapters 9-11
      4. To read chapters 9-11

Activity #1
      Give students ten minutes or so to work on their journal entries.

Activity #2
      Give students a few minutes to formulate answers for the study guide questions for chapters 7-8, and then discuss the answers to the questions in detail. Write the answers on the board or overhead transparency so students can have the correct answers for study purposes.

Activity #3
      Give students ten to fifteen minutes to look over the study questions and do the vocabulary work for chapters 9-11.

Activity #4
      Have students read chapters 9-11 silently in class. If students do not finish reading this section in class, they should do so prior to the next class period.

LESSON NINE

<u>Objectives</u>
       1. To give students time to work on their journal entries
       2. To review the main ideas and events from chapters 9-11
       3. To do the prereading work for chapter 12
       4. To read chapter 12

<u>Activity #1</u>
    Give students ten minutes or so to work on their journal entries.

<u>Activity #2</u>
    Give students a few minutes to formulate answers for the study guide questions for chapters 9-11, and then discuss the answers to the questions in detail. Write the answers on the board or overhead transparency.

<u>Activity #3</u>
    Give students ten to fifteen minutes to look over the study questions and do the vocabulary work for chapter 12.

<u>Activity #4</u>
    Have students read chapter 12 silently in class. If students do not finish reading this section in class, they should do so prior to the next class period.

LESSON TEN

<u>Objectives</u>
    1. To give students time to work on their journal entries
    2. To review the main ideas and events from chapter 12
    3. To discuss *Lord of the Flies* on interpretive and critical levels

<u>Activity #1</u>
    Give students about ten minutes to work on their journal entries.

<u>Activity #2</u>
    Take a few minutes at the beginning of the period to review the study questions for chapter 12.

<u>Activity #3</u>
    Choose the questions from the Extra Discussion Questions/Writing Assignments which seem most appropriate for your students. A class discussion of these questions is most effective if students have been given the opportunity to formulate answers to the questions prior to the discussion. To this end, you may either have all the students formulate answers to all the questions, divide your class into groups and assign one or more questions to each group, or you could assign one question to each student in your class. The option you choose will make a difference in the amount of class time needed for this activity.

<u>Activity #4</u>
    After students have had ample time to formulate answers to the questions, begin your class discussion of the questions and the ideas presented by the questions. Be sure students take notes during the discussion so they have information to study for the unit test.

EXTRA WRITING ASSIGNMENTS/DISCUSSION QUESTIONS - *Lord of the Flies*

Interpretation

1. From what point of view is the story told? How does that affect our understanding of the story?

2. If you were to rewrite *Lord of the Flies* as a play, where would you start and end each act? Explain why.

3. Are the characters in *Lord of the Flies* stereotypes? If so, explain why William Golding used stereotypes. If not, explain how the characters merit individuality.

4. Where is the climax of the story? Justify your answer.

5. Explain the importance of the setting in *Lord of the Flies*. Could this story have been set in a different time and place and still have the same effect?

6. In what ways does William Golding try to make the story believable? Is he successful; is the story believable?

7. Describe the meetings the boys had. When and why did they stop having meetings?

8. What are the conflicts in the story, and how is each resolved?

Critical

9. Compare and contrast Ralph and Jack.

10. What is the symbolic importance of the pig's head?

11. What is the symbolic importance of the shelters, the sand castles, the boys' physical appearances, and the beastie?

12. Evaluate William Golding's style of writing. How does it contribute to the value of the novel?

13. According to Mr. Golding, is evil intrinsic or extrinsic to humans?

14. What is the symbolic importance of each of the following: Piggy's glasses, the conch and the fire?

15. Why did the Lord of the Flies speak to Simon instead of any of the other boys?

16. Explain how the title relates to the events of the novel and the themes of *Lord of the Flies.*

17. Compare Jack's tactics to terrorist and gang tactics. How are they similar?

18. In the struggle for power between Jack and Ralph, what advantages does Jack have? Ralph?

19. Why did the boys consider Simon to be an animal as they made him their prey?

20. How do Piggy and Ralph attempt to rationalize their participation in the death of Simon? Contrast that with Jack and his group's reaction to their own participation.

21. How is *Lord of the Flies* two stories told at the same time?

22. Is *Lord of the Flies* a tragedy? If so, how? If not, why not?

23. Compare and contrast Piggy and Roger as the seconds to the leaders.

24. Explain the symbolism in the descriptions of the bodies of Simon and the pilot going out to sea.

25. Why did the boys build the fire on the mountaintop, and how could this have been symbolically important?

26. What symbolic relationship could the forest and Rock Castle have?

27. "'Run away,' said the head silently, 'go back to the others, It was a joke really -- why should you bother? You were just wrong, that's all. A little headache, something you ate, perhaps. Go back, child,' said the head silently." What does that mean?

28. "The [pig's] half-shut eyes were dim with the infinite cynicism of adult life." Explain.

29. Compare and contrast the deaths of Simon and Piggy.

30. Why did the "little boy who wore the remains of an extraordinary black cap on his red hair and who carried the remains of a pair of spectacles at his waist" start forward, then change his mind and stand still? Who was that boy? Why were the details of a <u>black</u> cap and <u>red</u> hair included?

31. Eating meat was important to the boys. Why? How was it symbolically important?

32. What is a parable, and how is *Lord of the Flies* one?

33. Ralph answers, "Yes" to the naval officer when he asks if a war is going on. Explain what the war is about and who the rival sides are.

34. Which characters in the book die? Who is responsible for each of their deaths?

Critical/Personal Response
35. What faults in our society does William Golding point out in *Lord of the Flies*?

36. Suppose the naval officer had not come along in the end, and Ralph had been murdered. How would that have changed the meaning of the story?

37. Traditionally, children are portrayed as innocent. Are they in *Lord of the Flies*? Explain how so or how not.

38. Whose fault was it that things didn't work out on the island?

39. In what way does the fact that the people on the island are children affect the story?

Personal Response
40. Did you enjoy reading *Lord of the Flies*? Why or why not?

41. If you were the leader of the boys in the beginning of the story, what would you have done differently that might have made things come out differently in the end?

42. If you were on the island with the boys, which character from the story do you think you would most likely be?

43. Suppose the story had been written in the first person narrative from Simon's point of view. How would it have been different?

<u>LESSON ELEVEN</u>

<u>Objectives</u>
     1. To give students time to work on their journal entries
     2. To review all of the vocabulary work done in this unit

<u>Activity</u>
     Choose one (or more) of the vocabulary review activities listed below and spend your class period as directed in the activity. Some of the materials for these review activities are located in the Vocabulary Resources section of this unit.

VOCABULARY REVIEW ACTIVITIES

1. Divide your class into two teams and have an old-fashioned spelling or definition bee.

2. Give each of your students (or students in groups of two, three or four) a *Lord of the Flies* Vocabulary Word Search Puzzle. The person (group) to find all of the vocabulary words in the puzzle first wins.

3. Give students a *Lord of the Flies* Vocabulary Word Search Puzzle without the word list. The person or group to find the most vocabulary words in the puzzle wins.

4. Use a *Lord of the Flies* Vocabulary Crossword Puzzle. Put the puzzle onto a transparency on the overhead projector (so everyone can see it), and do the puzzle together as a class.

5. Give students a *Lord of the Flies* Vocabulary Matching Worksheet to do.

6. Divide your class into two teams. Use the *Lord of the Flies* vocabulary words with their letters jumbled as a word list. Student 1 from Team A faces off against Student 1 from Team B. You write the first jumbled word on the board. The first student (1A or 1B) to unscramble the word wins the chance for his/her team to score points. If 1A wins the jumble, go to student 2A and give him/her a definition. He/she must give you the correct spelling of the vocabulary word which fits that definition. If he/she does, Team A scores a point, and you give student 3A a definition for which you expect a correctly spelled matching vocabulary word. Continue giving Team A definitions until some team member makes an incorrect response. An incorrect response sends the game back to the jumbled-word face off, this time with students 2A and 2B. Instead of repeating giving definitions to the first few students of each team, continue with the student after the one who gave the last incorrect response on the team. For example, if Team B wins the jumbled-word face-off, and student 5B gave the last incorrect answer for Team B, you would start this round of definition questions with student 6B, and so on. The team with the most points wins!

7. Have students write a story in which they correctly use as many vocabulary words as possible. Have students read their compositions orally! Post the most original compositions on your bulletin board!

LESSON TWELVE

Objectives
1. To give students time to work on their journal entries
2. To give students the opportunity to practice writing to inform.
3. To give the teacher the opportunity to evaluate students' writing skills.
4. To help students organize their nonfiction information for their oral presentations

Activity
Distribute Writing Assignment #2. Discuss the directions orally in detail. Allow the remaining class time for students to complete the activity.

Follow-Up: After you have graded the assignments, have a writing conference with the students. (This unit schedules one in Lesson Fifteen.) After the writing conference, allow students to revise their papers using your suggestions and corrections. Give them about three days from the date they receive their papers to complete the revision. I suggest grading the revisions on an A-C-E scale (all revisions well-done, some revisions made, few or no revisions made). This will speed your grading time and still give some credit for the students' efforts.

WRITING ASSIGNMENT #2 - *Lord of the Flies*

PROMPT

You have read at least one article of nonfiction relating to *Lord of the Flies*. Now you are to write a composition in which you summarize your article(s). This is to help you review the information as well as to help prepare you for your oral presentation.

PREWRITING

Your reading has been done, and you probably have some notes on paper sitting in front of you. Look at your notes and begin to organize them. Arrange the notes in an order that makes sense: chronological order (order of time that the events happen) is often appropriate.

DRAFTING

Start with a paragraph in which you introduce your topic. In the body of your paper write your summary. Finally, write a paragraph in which you give your opinions about your topic (tell whether you agree or disagree with the article, for example).

PROMPT

When you finish the rough draft of your paper, ask a student who sits near you to read it. After reading your rough draft, he/she should tell you what he/she liked best about your work, which parts were difficult to understand, and ways in which your work could be improved. Reread your paper considering your critic's comments, and make the corrections you think are necessary.

PROOFREADING

Do a final proofreading of your paper double-checking your grammar, spelling, organization, and the clarity of your ideas.

LESSON THIRTEEN

Objectives
1. To give students time to work on their journal entries
2. To instruct students in basic camping and survival skills
3. To give students a real-life application relating to the novel

Activity #1
Give students about ten minutes to work on their journal entries.

Activity #2
Invite a local Boy Scout (or Girl Scout) leader to come in to your classroom and discuss camping and survival techniques. He (or she) should be sure to include information about basic equipment and skills, some "tricks of the trade" for surviving in the wilderness without modern conveniences.

LESSON FOURTEEN

Objectives
1. To give students time to work on their journals.
2. To have students practice public speaking
3. To enrich students' understanding of our world

Activity #1
Give students about ten minutes to work on their journal entries.

Activity #2
Ask each student to give a brief oral report about the nonfiction work he/she read for the nonfiction reading assignment. Your criteria for evaluating this report will vary depending on the level of your students. You may wish for students to give a complete report without using notes of any kind, or you may want students to read directly from a written report, or you may want to do something in between these two extremes. Just make students aware of your criteria in ample time for them to prepare their reports.

Start with one student's report. After that, ask if anyone else in the class has read about a topic related to the first student's report. If no one has, choose another student at random. After each report, be sure to ask if anyone has a report related to the one just completed. That will help keep a continuity during the discussion of the reports.

LESSON FIFTEEN

Objectives
1. To give students the opportunity to practice writing to persuade
2. To review the events of the stories and the motives of the characters.
3. To give the teacher a chance to evaluate students' individual writing
4. To give students time to work on their journal entries.

Activity #1

Distribute Writing Assignment #3. Discuss the directions orally in detail. Allow the remaining class time for students to complete the activity.

NOTE: While students are working on Writing Assignment #3, call students to your desk (or some other private area) to discuss their papers from Writing Assignment 2. A Writing Evaluation Form is included with this unit to help structure your conferences.

Follow-Up: Follow up as in Writing Assignment 2, allowing students to correct their errors and turn in the revision for credit. A good time for your next writing conferences would be the day following the unit test.

Activity #2

If students complete the writing assignment early, they should use the remaining time to work on their journal entries.

WRITING EVALUATION FORM - *Lord of the Flies*

Name _____ Date _____

Writing Assignment #1 for the *Lord of the Flies* unit   Grade _____

Circle One For Each Item:

Grammar: correct   errors noted on paper

Spelling: correct   errors noted on paper

Punctuation: correct   errors noted on paper

Legibility: excellent   good   fair   poor

_____

_____

Strengths:

Weaknesses:

Comments/Suggestions:

WRITING ASSIGNMENT #3 - *Lord of the Flies*

PROMPT

The boys didn't get along very well, did they. Well, suppose you were sent in to straighten things out. Pretend you are a mediator sent in to smooth things over between the two main groups of boys. Your assignment is to persuade the boys to get along better. You have called them all together for a meeting, and the composition you write is the speech you will give to the boys persuading them to get along with each other.

PREWRITING

First of all, what went wrong? Why are the boys fighting with each other? What are the basic, underlying problems causing the friction? What will happen if the boys continue their present course? What do the boys have to gain by getting along better? Jot down your answers to these questions on a piece of paper.

DRAFTING

Begin with an introductory paragraph. Introduce yourself and why you have gathered the boys for this meeting.

In the body of your composition (speech), write a paragraph to show the boys that, in fact, a problem exists (in case they don't realize it). Write a paragraph explaining what will happen if they continue their course of action. Give graphic examples where possible. Write a paragraph pointing out what the boys have to gain by getting along better. Again, use graphic examples where possible. Write a paragraph explaining the underlying problems causing the situation. Finally, offer a paragraph of possible solutions which would help to eliminate the underlying problems causing the situation.

End your composition with a concluding paragraph in which you summarize your main points, give the boys encouragement to adopt and attain this goal of peace, and thank the boys for their efforts and attention.

PROMPT

When you finish the rough draft of your paper, ask a student who sits near you to read it. After reading your rough draft, he/she should tell you what he/she liked best about your work, which parts were difficult to understand, and ways in which your work could be improved. Reread your paper considering your critic's comments, and make the corrections you think are necessary.

PROOFREADING

Do a final proofreading of your paper double-checking your grammar, spelling, organization, and the clarity of your ideas.

LESSONS SIXTEEN AND SEVENTEEN

Objectives

1. To show students a film interpretation of *Lord of the Flies*
2. To stimulate students' critical thinking
3. To reward students for all their good work during the unit
4. To set up a discussion for Lesson Seventeen

Activity

Show a film version of *Lord of the Flies*. Ask your students to pay particular attention to the movie to try to find any differences between the film version and the text. Also, tell students to take notes about the characters and scenes, about things they visualized differently as they read from how they appeared on the screen.

LESSON EIGHTEEN

Objectives

1. To compare and contrast the film *Lord of the Flies* with the text
2. To give students time to complete their journal entries

Activity #1

Tell students to get out their notes they have made during the last two class periods. Begin with a general question like, "What did you think of the film?" and see what kinds of responses you get. Go, then to more specific questions: Did the film follow the plot in the book exactly? Was Simon exactly the way you visualized him when you read the book? etc.

Activity #2

After you have completed your discussion of the film, give students the remainder of the class period to complete their journal entries. Remind students that their journals must be ready for grading in your next class period.

LESSON NINETEEN

Objectives
1. To bring Writing Assignment #1 to a close
2. To give students a chance to show off their journals
3. To have some fun

Activity #1
Tell students to take about five minutes to choose their favorite journal entry and prepare an oral statement which will give enough background information that all students in the class will understand it.

Activity #2
Have students take turns telling the class about their favorite journal entries. Students should give a brief statement to "set up" the situation and then read the entry as they have written it.

NOTE: If your students have been treating their time on the island in a realistic manner, today is a good day to show off projects they have created, for them to be "rescued" (perhaps "hire" a few students from another class to come in and role-play the rescuers), and to generally bring the unit to a conclusion. If you are awarding prizes (props merchants have donated for your room, for example) for the best journal entries, etc. today would be a good day to make those awards, or you could wait and do it after the unit test in Lesson Twenty-One.

LESSON TWENTY

Objective
To review the main ideas presented in *Lord of the Flies*

Activity #1
Choose one of the review games/activities included in this packet and spend your class period as outlined there. Some materials for these activities are located in the Unit Resources section of this unit.

Activity #2
Remind students that the Unit Test will be in the next class meeting. Stress the review of the Study Guides and their class notes as a last minute, brush-up review for homework.

REVIEW GAMES/ACTIVITIES - *Lord of the Flies*

1. Ask the class to make up a unit test for *Lord of the Flies*. The test should have 4 sections: matching, true/false, short answer, and essay. Students may use 1/2 period to make the test and then swap papers and use the other 1/2 class period to take a test a classmate has devised. (open book) You may want to use the unit test included in this packet or take questions from the students' unit tests to formulate your own test.

2. Take 1/2 period for students to make up true and false questions (including the answers). Collect the papers and divide the class into two teams. Draw a big tic-tac-toe board on the chalk board. Make one team X and one team O. Ask questions to each side, giving each student one turn. If the question is answered correctly, that students' team's letter (X or O) is placed in the box. If the answer is incorrect, no mark is placed in the box. The object is to get three marks in a row like tic-tac-toe. You may want to keep track of the number of games won for each team.

3. Take 1/2 period for students to make up questions (true/false and short answer). Collect the questions. Divide the class into two teams. You'll alternate asking questions to individual members of teams A & B (like in a spelling bee). The question keeps going from A to B until it is correctly answered, then a new question is asked. A correct answer does not allow the team to get another question. Correct answers are +2 points; incorrect answers are -1 point.

4. Have students pair up and quiz each other from their study guides and class notes.

5. Give students a *Lord of the Flies* crossword puzzle to complete.

6. Divide your class into two teams. Use the *Lord of the Flies* crossword words with their letters jumbled as a word list. Student 1 from Team A faces off against Student 1 from Team B. You write the first jumbled word on the board. The first student (1A or 1B) to unscramble the word wins the chance for his/her team to score points. If 1A wins the jumble, go to student 2A and give him/her a clue. He/she must give you the correct word which matches that clue. If he/she does, Team A scores a point, and you give student 3A a clue for which you expect another correct response. Continue giving Team A clues until some team member makes an incorrect response. An incorrect response sends the game back to the jumbled-word face off, this time with students 2A and 2B. Instead of repeating giving clues to the first few students of each team, continue with the student after the one who gave the last incorrect response on the team. For example, if Team B wins the jumbled-word face-off, and student 5B gave the last incorrect answer for Team B, you would start this round of clue questions with student 6B, and so on. The team with the most points wins!

UNIT TESTS

LESSON TWENTY-ONE

Objective
        To test the students understanding of the main ideas and themes in *Lord of the Flies*

Activity #1
        Distribute the unit tests. Go over the instructions in detail and allow the students the
entire class period to complete the exam.

NOTES ABOUT THE UNIT TESTS IN THIS UNIT:
        There are 5 different unit tests which follow.
        There are two short answer tests which are based primarily on facts from the novel.
        There is one advanced short answer unit test. It is based on the extra discussion questions
and quotations. Use the matching key for short answer unit test 2 to check the matching section
of the advanced short answer unit test. There is no key for the short answer questions and
quotations. The answers will be based on the discussions you have had during class.
        There are two multiple choice unit tests. Following the two unit tests, you will find an
answer sheet on which students should mark their answers. The same answer sheet should be
used for both tests; however, students' answers will be different for each test. Following the
students' answer sheet for the multiple choice tests you will find your answer keys.
        The short answer tests have a vocabulary section. You should choose 10 of the
vocabulary words from this unit, read them orally and have the students write them down. Then,
either have students write a definition or use the words in sentences.

        Use these words for the vocabulary section of the advanced short answer unit test:

inscrutable	skewed	gesticulated
impervious	hiatus	rebuke
maternal	apex	improvisation

Activity #2
        Collect all test papers and assigned books prior to the end of the class period.

SHORT ANSWER UNIT TEST 1 - *Lord of the Flies*

I. Matching/Identify

___ 1. Ralph   a. numerous small children of the group
___ 2. Piggy   b. Sam's brother
___ 3. Simon   c. poetic, sensitive loner
___ 4. Jack   d. "slight, furtive," natural tendency to cruelty
___ 5. Sam   e. choir leader, "silly without ugliness"
___ 6. Maurice   f. intelligent, not very active
___ 7. Roger   g. handsome, athletic, natural leader
___ 8. Littluns   h. one of the pair of identical twins
___ 9. Eric   i. "grinning all the time," choir boy

II. Short Answer

1. How did the boys happen to come to the island?

2. What do the boys have that is the symbol of authority in the society they form?

3. Why does the boys' plan for rescue fail?

4. Although Ralph criticizes the boys for their lack of cooperation, does he bear some of the responsibility for the failures of the group to achieve its goals? Why or why not?

5. What causes the hunters, who had promised to keep the fire burning, to neglect it and allow it to go out?

6. Why does Jack paint his face?

7. Compare Ralph's treatment of the littluns with Jack's.

8. To what does Ralph's demonstration of his hunting prowess lead?

9. Although he is not able to get the boys to vote Ralph out of office as chief, Jack manages to overthrow Ralph's authority anyway. How?

10. Describe Simon's strange encounter with the Lord of the Flies.

11. What happens to the conch and to Piggy?

12. What or who saves Ralph in the end?

II. Essay

Choose another title for the book and explain why your title is appropriate in terms of the themes and ideas presented by the author.

IV. Vocabulary

   Listen to the vocabulary words and spell them. After you have spelled all the words, go back and write down the definitions.

   1.

   2.

   3.

   4.

   5.

   6.

   7.

   8.

   9.

   10.

SHORT ANSWER UNIT TEST 2 - *Lord of the Flies*

I. Matching

___ 1. Ralph
___ 2. Piggy
___ 3. Simon
___ 4. Jack
___ 5. Sam
___ 6. Maurice
___ 7. Roger
___ 8. Littluns
___ 9. Eric

a. poetic, sensitive loner
b. one of the pair of identical twins
c. numerous small children of the group
d. choir leader, "silly without ugliness"
e. "slight, furtive," natural tendency to cruelty
f. handsome, athletic, natural leader
g. "grinning all the time," choir boy
h. Sam's brother
i. intelligent, not very active

II. Short Answer

1. What do the boys have that is the symbol of authority in the society they form?

2. Why does Jack hesitate when he lifts his knife to kill the piglet, and what does he promise will happen next time he meets a pig?

3. Although Ralph criticizes the boys for their lack of cooperation, does he bear some of the responsibility for the failures of the group to achieve its goals? Why or why not?

4. What is Simon saying when he thinks the "beast" may be inside they boys themselves?

5. Although he is not able to get the boys to vote Ralph out of office as chief, Jack manages to overthrow Ralph's authority anyway. How?

6. What happens to the conch and to Piggy?

7. What is Ralph's reaction when he encounters the pig's skull?

III. Composition

Answer each of the following questions with a complete paragraph:

1. What are the conflicts in the story, and how is each resolved?

2. Explain the symbolic importance of the pig's head, the shelters, the sand castles, Piggy's glasses, and the fire.

3. "'Run away,' said the head silently, 'go back to the others, It was a joke really -- why should you bother? You were just wrong, that's all. A little headache, something you ate, perhaps. Go back, child,' said the head silently." What does that mean?

IV. Vocabulary

Listen to the vocabulary words and spell them. After you have spelled all the words, go back and write down the definitions.

1.

2.

3.

4.

5.

6.

7.

8.

9.

10.

KEY: SHORT ANSWER UNIT TESTS - *Lord of the Flies*

The short answer questions are taken directly from the study guides.
If you need to look up the answers, you will find them in the study guide section.

Answers to the composition questions will vary depending on your
class discussions and the level of your students.

For the vocabulary section of the test, choose ten of the
words from the vocabulary lists to read orally for your students.

The answers to the matching section of the test are below.

Answers to the matching section of the Advanced Short Answer Unit Test
are the same as for Short Answer Unit Test #2.

Test #1	Test #2
1. G	1. F
2. F	2. I
3. C	3. A
4. E	4. D
5. H	5. B
6. I	6. G
7. D	7. E
8. A	8. C
9. B	9. H

ADVANCED SHORT ANSWER UNIT TEST - *Lord of the Flies*

I. Matching

___ 1. Ralph
___ 2. Piggy
___ 3. Simon
___ 4. Jack
___ 5. Sam
___ 6. Maurice
___ 7. Roger
___ 8. Littluns
___ 9. Eric

a. poetic, sensitive loner
b. one of the pair of identical twins
c. numerous small children of the group
d. choir leader, "silly without ugliness"
e. "slight, furtive," natural tendency to cruelty
f. handsome, athletic, natural leader
g. "grinning all the time," choir boy
h. Sam's brother
i. intelligent, not very active

II. Composition

1. Where is the climax of the story? Justify your answer.

2. What are the conflicts in the story, and how is each resolved?

3. Compare and contrast Ralph and Jack.

4. What is the symbolic importance of the pig's head, the beastie, Piggy's glasses, the conch, and the fire?

5. Why did the Lord of the Flies speak to Simon instead of any of the other boys?

6. How is *Lord of the Flies* two stories told at the same time?

7. Compare and contrast Piggy and Roger as the seconds to the leaders.

8. Why did the boys build the fire on the mountaintop, and how could this have been symbolically important?

9. "'Run away,' said the head silently, 'go back to the others, It was a joke really -- why should you bother? You were just wrong, that's all. A little headache, something you ate, perhaps. Go back, child,' said the head silently." What does that mean?

10. "The [pig's] half-shut eyes were dim with the infinite cynicism of adult life." Explain.

11. Compare and contrast the deaths of Simon and Piggy.

III. Essay

What lessons should we learn from reading *Lord of the Flies*?
Be specific, and support your statements with specific examples from the text.

IV. Vocabulary

Listen to the vocabulary words and write them down. Go back later and write a composition using all of the words. The composition must in some way relate to *Lord of the Flies*.

MULTIPLE CHOICE UNIT TEST 1 - *Lord of the Flies*

I. Matching

___ 1. Ralph
___ 2. Piggy
___ 3. Simon
___ 4. Jack
___ 5. Sam
___ 6. Maurice
___ 7. Roger
___ 8. Littluns
___ 9. Eric

a. numerous small children of the group
b. Sam's brother
c. poetic, sensitive loner
d. "slight, furtive," natural tendency to cruelty
e. choir leader, "silly without ugliness"
f. intelligent, not very active
g. handsome, athletic, natural leader
h. one of the pair of identical twins
i. "grinning all the time," choir boy

II. Multiple Choice

1. What do the boys have that is the symbol of authority in the society they form?
   A. A conch shell
   B. A British flag
   C. A Bible
   D. A whale jaw bone

2. Who are the hunters, and what is their job?
   A. The littluns; looking for ships and planes
   B. Samneric; killing dangerous animals
   C. The choirboys; getting food
   D. Simon, Piggy, Ralph; governing the boys

3. Although Ralph criticizes the boys for their lack of cooperation, does he bear some of the responsibility for the failures of the group to achieve its goals?
   A. Ralph is partially responsible. He has the desire to bring civilization, but lacks the competence to do so. He believes life is too much like a story-book.
   B. Ralph is not responsible at all. He has done all he could to get the boys to cooperate, and they have chosen not to.
   C. Ralph bears a large part of the responsibility. He is not using his natural leadership abilities in a way that is in the best interests of the whole group.
   D. Ralph bears only a very small part of the responsibility. He is really much too shy and fearful to be able to organize the boys.

4. After Maurice and Roger destroy the littluns' sand castles, Roger stalks the young boy named Henry. When he begins to throw stones, why does Roger just throw near Henry instead of directly at him?
    A. Roger is scared off by a noise in the jungle behind him.
    B. Roger is afraid that the littluns will hit back.
    C. Maurice tells Roger he will beat him up if he hits any of the littluns.
    D. The old laws of school, church, and family still hold him back.

5. What causes the hunters, who had promised to keep the fire burning, to neglect it and allow it to go out?
    A. They become more interested in trying to build a canoe.
    B. They are becoming more savage, and can only think about hunting.
    C. They think that the other boys will get over their fear of the dark better if there is no light at all for a few nights.
    D. They are inexperienced and don't really know how to keep it burning.

6. Why does Jack paint his face?
    A. The paint protects his sensitive skin from the sun.
    B. He thinks it will cheer up the others.
    C. He uses the paint as a mask to blot out his real self and become a savage.
    D. He tries to scare the littluns into obeying him.

7. Compare Ralph's treatment of the littluns with Jack's.
    A. Ralph tries to calm their fears and give them a sense of security. Jack intimidates and frightens them.
    B. Ralph treats them harshly, thinking it is for their own good. Jack protects them and makes sure they have enough to eat.
    C. Ralph is kind and understanding. Jack fears the littluns will like Ralph better, so he tries to win them by being kinder than Ralph, although it is a false kindness.
    D. Neither Ralph nor Jack have much experience with younger children. They soon tire of the littluns' immaturity and ignore them.

8. What is Simon saying when he thinks the "beast" may be inside the boys themselves?
    A. They have eaten some poisoned meat.
    B. None of them are really human.
    C. The dark side of the human personality can destroy mankind.
    D. It is all in their imaginations.

9. To what does Ralph's demonstration of his hunting prowess lead?
    A. It re-establishes him as the leader, and the boys rekindle the signal fire.
    B. It makes the littluns afraid of him and they run and hide.
    C. Jack realizes Ralph's strength and vows to fight him.
    D. The boys go into a hunting frenzy and begin jabbing and poking at Robert.

10. How does Jack overthrow Ralph's authority?
    A. Jack gets the boys to vote Ralph out of office.
    B. Jack tells the others he is the oldest, and the oldest should rule.
    C. Jack announces he won't play anymore, and goes off by himself.
    D. Jack challenges Ralph to a spear-throwing contest and wins.

11. What is the meaning of the Lord of the Flies' message to Simon?
    A. Evil is a trait inside of man.
    B. Dreams can be more powerful than reality.
    C. It is unhealthy to eat uncooked meat.
    D. If they ignore the beast it will go away.

12. Who or what is the Lord of the Flies?
    A. It is the name they have given the dead pilot.
    B. It is a large, poisonous insect that thrives on the island.
    C. It is a game the littluns play to pass the time.
    D. It is the sow's head, and represents evil.

13. What happens to Simon when he returns to the group?
    A. He keeps quiet because he knows they won't believe him.
    B. He joins in the dance and becomes evil himself.
    C. He tells Ralph the truth, and then goes off to live alone.
    D. The hunters kill him before he can tell them anything.

14. What happens to the conch and Piggy?
    A. Piggy steals the conch and escapes into the jungle.
    B. They are both eaten by a wild boar.
    C. Piggy saves the conch but loses his glasses.
    D. They are both shattered by the huge boulder.

15. How is Ralph saved in the end?
    A. The littluns push Jack off the mountain top into the sea.
    B. He is stronger than Jack and defeats him.
    C. He swims to the safety of another island.
    D. A British naval officer finds him.

III. Composition

    Write three paragraphs, one for each of three themes that is present in *Lord of the Flies*. In each paragraph use specific examples from the text to support your statements.

IV. Vocabulary

1. EXCRUCIATINGLY		A. Tall, pointed formations
2. PINNACLES		B. Thick underbrush providing cover
3. PROPITATINGLY		C. Intensely painfully
4. INIMICAL		D. Plausible but actually false
5. CREPITATION		E. Obscured; blocked from view
6. SKEWED		F. Turned to one side
7. PURGED		G. To criticize or reprimand
8. COVERTS		H. A gloomy effect
9. TEMPESTUOUSLY		I. Appeasingly; trying to please
10. REBUKE		J. Impenetrable
11. BASTION		K. Intangible; not perceived by touch
12. GESTICULATED		L. Having rich or profuse growth
13. INSCRUTABLE		M. Relating to motherhood
14. OPAQUE		N. A well-fortified position
15. SPECIOUS		O. Light can't get through it
16. PALL		P. Like a storm; turbulently
17. ECLIPSED		Q. Unfriendly; hostile
18. MATERNAL		R. Freed from impurities
19. LUXURIANCE		S. Crackling sound
20. IMPALPABLE		T. Made hand motions

MULTIPLE CHOICE UNIT TEST 2 - *Lord of the Flies*

I. Matching

___ 1. Ralph   a. poetic, sensitive loner
___ 2. Piggy   b. one of the pair of identical twins
___ 3. Simon   c. numerous small children of the group
___ 4. Jack   d. choir leader, "silly without ugliness"
___ 5. Sam   e. "slight, furtive," natural tendency to cruelty
___ 6. Maurice   f. handsome, athletic, natural leader
___ 7. Roger   g. "grinning all the time," choir boy
___ 8. Littluns   h. Sam's brother
___ 9. Eric   i. intelligent, not very active

II. Multiple Choice

1. What do the boys have that is the symbol of authority in the society they form?
   - A. A Bible
   - B. A British flag
   - C. A conch shell
   - D. A whale jaw bone

2. Who are the hunters, and what is their job?
   - A. The littluns; looking for ships and planes
   - B. Samneric; killing dangerous animals
   - C. Simon, Piggy, Ralph; governing the boys
   - D. The choirboys; getting food

3. Although Ralph criticizes the boys for their lack of cooperation, does he bear some of the responsibility for the failures of the group to achieve its goals?
   - A. Ralph is not responsible at all. He has done all he could to get the boys to cooperate, and they have chosen not to.
   - B. Ralph is partially responsible. He has the desire to bring civilization, but lacks the competence to do so. He believes life is too much like a story-book.
   - C. Ralph bears a large part of the responsibility. He is not using his natural leadership abilities in a way that is in the best interests of the whole group.
   - D. Ralph bears only a very small part of the responsibility. He is really much too shy and fearful to be able to organize the boys.

4. After Maurice and Roger destroy the littluns' sand castles, Roger stalks the young boy named Henry. When he begins to throw stones, why does Roger just throw near Henry instead of directly at him?
    A. The old laws of school, church, and family still hold him back.
    B. Roger is afraid that the littluns will hit back.
    C. Maurice tells Roger he will beat him up if he hits any of the littluns.
    D. Roger is scared off by a noise in the jungle behind him.

5. What causes the hunters, who had promised to keep the fire burning, to neglect it and allow it to go out?
    A. They become more interested in trying to build a canoe.
    B. They think that the other boys will get over their fear of the dark better if there is no light at all for a few nights.
    C. They are becoming more savage, and can only think about hunting.
    D. They are inexperienced and don't really know how to keep it burning.

6. Why does Jack paint his face?
    A. The paint protects his sensitive skin from the sun.
    B. He uses the paint as a mask to blot out his real self and become a savage.
    C. He thinks it will cheer up the others.
    D. He tries to scare the littluns into obeying him.

7. Compare Ralph's treatment of the littluns with Jack's.
    A. Neither Ralph nor Jack have much experience with younger children. They soon tire of the littluns' immaturity and ignore them.
    B. Ralph treats them harshly, thinking it is for their own good. Jack protects them and makes sure they have enough to eat.
    C. Ralph is kind and understanding. Jack fears the littluns will like Ralph better, so he tries to win them by being kinder than Ralph, although it is a false kindness.
    D. Ralph tries to calm their fears and give them a sense of security. Jack intimidates and frightens them.

8. What is Simon saying when he thinks the "beast" may be inside the boys themselves?
    A. They have eaten some poisoned meat.
    B. None of them are really human.
    C. It is all in their imaginations.
    D. The dark side of the human personality can destroy mankind.

9. To what does Ralph's demonstration of his hunting prowess lead?
   A. It re-establishes him as the leader, and the boys rekindle the signal fire.
   B. The boys go into a hunting frenzy and begin jabbing and poking at Robert.
   C. Jack realizes Ralph's strength and vows to fight him.
   D. It makes the littluns afraid of him and they run and hide.

10. How does Jack overthrow Ralph's authority?
   A. Jack announces he won't play anymore, and goes off by himself.
   B. Jack tells the others he is the oldest, and the oldest should rule.
   C. Jack gets the boys to vote Ralph out of office.
   D. Jack challenges Ralph to a spear-throwing contest and wins.

11. What is the meaning of the Lord of the Flies' message to Simon?
   A. Dreams can be more powerful than reality.
   B. Evil is a trait inside of man.
   C. It is unhealthy to eat uncooked meat.
   D. If they ignore the beast it will go away.

12. Who or what is the Lord of the Flies?
   A. It is the sow's head, and represents evil.
   B. It is a large, poisonous insect that thrives on the island.
   C. It is a game the littluns play to pass the time.
   D. It is the name they have given the dead pilot.

13. What happens to Simon when he returns to the group?
   A. He keeps quiet because he knows they won't believe him.
   B. He joins in the dance and becomes evil himself.
   C. The hunters kill him before he can tell them anything.
   D. He tells Ralph the truth, and then goes off to live alone.

14. What happens to the conch and Piggy?
   A. They are both shattered by the huge boulder.
   B. They are both eaten by a wild boar.
   C. Piggy saves the conch but loses his glasses.
   D. Piggy steals the conch and escapes into the jungle.

15. How is Ralph saved in the end?
   A. The littluns push Jack off the mountain top into the sea.
   B. He is stronger than Jack and defeats him.
   C. A British naval officer finds him.
   D. He swims to the safety of another island.

III. Composition

On the surface, *Lord of the Flies* is just a story about some boys stranded on an island. Explain the deeper meaning of the book using specific examples from the text.

IV. Vocabulary

1. TAUT	A. Without being spoken
2. TRUCULENTLY	B. A break
3. MYOPIA	C. A visual defect like nearsightedness
4. PURGED	D. Intensely painfully
5. PROPITATINGLY	E. Freed from impurities
6. INSCRUTABLE	F. Having rich or profuse growth
7. ASSIMILATING	G. Disposed to fight
8. GLAMOUR	H. Decorated
9. TACITLY	I. Tight
10. LUXURIANCE	J. Incapable of being affected
11. SANCTITY	K. Lean and muscular
12. ECLIPSED	L. A likeness or image
13. IMPERVIOUS	M. To criticize or reprimand
14. INCREDULITY	N. Sacredness; godliness
15. EXCRUCIATINGLY	O. Appeasingly; trying to please
16. REBUKE	P. Absorbing
17. EFFIGY	Q. Disbelief
18. FESTOONED	R. Impenetrable
19. SINEWY	S. Obscured; blocked from view
20. HIATUS	T. Magic spell; enchantment

ANSWER SHEET - *Lord of the Flies*
Multiple Choice Unit Tests

I. Matching	II. Multiple Choice	IV. Vocabulary
1. ____	1. ____	1. ____
2. ____	2. ____	2. ____
3. ____	3. ____	3. ____
4. ____	4. ____	4. ____
5. ____	5. ____	5. ____
6. ____	6. ____	6. ____
7. ____	7. ____	7. ____
8. ____	8. ____	8. ____
9. ____	9. ____	9. ____
	10. ____	10. ____
	11. ____	11. ____
	12. ____	12. ____
	13. ____	13. ____
	14. ____	14. ____
	15. ____	15. ____
		16. ____
		17. ____
		18. ____
		19. ____
		20. ____

MULTIPLE CHOICE UNIT TEST ANSWER KEYS - *Lord of the Flies*

Answers to Unit Test 1 are in the left column.. Answers to Unit Test 2 are in the right column.

I. Matching		II. Multiple Choice		IV. Vocabulary	
1. G	F	1. A	C	1. C	I
2. F	I	2. C	D	2. A	G
3. C	A	3. A	B	3. I	C
4. E	D	4. D	A	4. Q	E
5. H	B	5. B	C	5. S	O
6. I	G	6. C	B	6. F	R
7. D	E	7. A	D	7. R	P
8. A	C	8. C	D	8. B	T
9. B	H	9. D	B	9. P	A
		10. C	A	10. G	F
		11. A	B	11. N	N
		12. D	A	12. T	S
		13. D	C	13. J	J
		14. D	A	14. O	Q
		15. D	C	15. D	D
				16. H	M
				17. E	L
				18. M	H
				19. L	K
				20. K	B

UNIT RESOURCE MATERIALS

BULLETIN BOARD IDEAS - *Lord of the Flies*

1. Save one corner of the board for the best of students' *Lord of the Flies* writing assignments.

2. Title the board, "LORD OF THE FLIES: MAN'S INHUMANITY TO MAN." Have students bring in visual examples of ways people are cruel to each other. Discuss each and have students post their own examples on the bulletin board.

3. Title the board, "LORD OF THE FLIES: MASKS." Post examples of different kinds of masks people use today: from ceremonial masks to things we symbolically hide behind.

4. Take one of the word search puzzles from the extra activities packet and with a marker copy it over in a large size on the bulletin board. Write the clue words to find to one side. Invite students prior to and after class to find the words and circle them on the bulletin board.

5. Do a bulletin board about careers related to the airline industry, camping, the wilderness, social psychology, psychology, social work, the food industry, weapons/hunting, etc.

6. Title the board, "LORD OF THE FLIES: WHAT IT MEANS TO BE CIVILIZED." Have each student write one idea about "What it means to be civilized" on background paper on the board. Discuss each idea.

7. Title the board, "MANKIND: GOOD OR EVIL?" Post pictures of both good works and bad things people do. Use the board as a springboard for discussion of the topic.

8. Write several of the most significant quotations from the book onto the board on brightly colored paper.

9. Make a bulletin board listing the vocabulary words for this unit. As you complete sections of the novel and discuss the vocabulary for each section, write the definitions on the bulletin board. (If your board is one students face frequently, it will help them learn the words.)

10. Make a bulletin board relating to survival skills. Perhaps your guest speaker could help provide some materials.

EXTRA ACTIVITIES - *Lord of the Flies*

One of the difficulties in teaching a novel is that all students don't read at the same speed. One student who likes to read may take the book home and finish it in a day or two. Sometimes a few students finish the in-class assignments early. The problem, then, is finding suitable extra activities for students.

The best thing I've found is to keep a little library in the classroom. For this unit on *Lord of the Flies,* you might check out from the school library other related books and articles about survival skills, camping, hunting, psychology, social psychology, the food industry, or careers in any of those related fields. Articles of criticism about *Lord of the Flies*, the text or the movie, would be interesting for some students. Biographical information about the author or other works by the author would also be good to have on hand.

Other things you may keep on hand are puzzles. We have made some relating directly to *Lord of the Flies* for you. Feel free to duplicate them.

Some students may like to draw. You might devise a contest or allow some extra-credit grade for students who draw characters or scenes from *Lord of the Flies*. Note, too, that if the students do not want to keep their drawings you may pick up some extra bulletin board materials this way. If you have a contest and you supply the prize (a CD or something like that perhaps), you could, possibly, make the drawing itself a non-refundable entry fee.

The pages which follow contain games, puzzles and worksheets. The keys, when appropriate, immediately follow the puzzle or worksheet. There are two main groups of activities: one group for the unit; that is, generally relating to the *Lord of the Flies* text, and another group of activities related strictly to the *Lord of the Flies* vocabulary.

Directions for these games, puzzles and worksheets are self-explanatory. The object here is to provide you with extra materials you may use in any way you choose.

MORE ACTIVITIES - *Lord of the Flies*

1. Pick a chapter or scene with a great deal of dialogue and have the students act it out on a stage. (Perhaps you could assign various scenes to different groups of students so more than one scene could be acted and more students could participate.)

2. See the list of bulletin board ideas for activities related to bulletin boards.

3. Have students create a game in which they use the settings and the characters from *Lord of the Flies*.

4. Have students design a book cover (front and back and inside flaps) for *Lord of the Flies*.

5. Have students design a bulletinboard (ready to be put up; not just sketched) for *Lord of the Flies*.

6. Have students research and report on any of the topics listed for suggested extra reading.

7. Have students each research about different civilizations that have come and gone through the centuries. Students should explain approximately when the civilization started, if known, its customs, rules, rulers, etc., and when and why it failed.

8. Have students discuss or write what happens to these boys when they return to civilization. How will their lives be different? How will they have to readjust? Will they be able to readjust?

9. Invite a social psychologist to visit your class to discuss the dynamics of the civilization and the personalities of the characters in *Lord of the Flies*.

10. If you live in an area where young people often go hunting with (or without) their parents, hold a mini-course on hunting safety.

WORD SEARCH - *Lord of the Flies*

All words in this list are associated with *Lord of the Flies*. The words are placed backwards, forward, diagonally, up and down. The included words are listed below the word searches.

```
F S D R N Q T T C C V Z K Z D M K S V F G K H L
L E K Y C P B H P H A H S G C F S F E S B Y Y N
C V R U S X I H Z L C N R F R S N F R N P N M S
K N G I L E P L S N A F D E E I W G R O O E E P
C L I F F L A T O C O Y E L C O N F L I C T A X
L R W A A O L C I R G M T A E I Y K T A A K S R
P M Y R T U R R F G D S I G R S F A F T S H W V
E C N A D N E E I R A I N S K D R F I G W S C C
M E W A L N U P S C P T N C A E A S O M O O E D
C P N J M S M O V T C U A B P V E R Y H R O O S
V T B A P G W A M N E J G O E H A B K P I B D D
G R S H L L F Y U L N C O J H A O G S N F D T G
B O D C K P H S T R T C P R F U S E E M E F E M
C P L Y B R R T H X I Y P D L D D T L F P S T Y
C R L D Y P I I C G D C M D Q T L H I M S W S Z
M L L Y I L B Q A V S R E T N U H G R E H F Q X
Z C Z Y D N K H N T Q R Z W B T D T G X Y T Y K
V K S T Q R G S F R L Y F N Q S P R G T Y C C F
M W T D Z N Q Y H N S S F G V V C N H B R H B W
Z J W X Q T L P Y Q N N Q C H B J L H Z M R D P
```

ADULTS	CRY	HAIR	RAIN
AIRPLANE	DANCE	HESITATES	RALPH
BEASTIE	DARKNESS	HIDE	ROCK
BOULDER	FACE	HUNTERS	SAMNERIC
CANDLE	FEAR	JACK	SAVAGE
CASTLE	FIRE	LORD	SEA
CHIEF	FLAT	MAURICE	SIMON
CLIFF	FOREST	MOUNTAIN	SKULL
CONCH	GLASSES	OFFICER	SPEAR
CONFLICT	GOLDING	PIGGY	STONES
COOPERATION	GOOD	PLAY	SUN
CORPSE	GRIN		WOOD

CROSSWORD - *Lord of the Flies*

CROSSWORD CLUES - *Lord of the Flies*

ACROSS

1. There are no _____ on the island until the officer arrives
5. Jack slashed the green _____ buds
9. It shatters the conch and Piggy
11. Choir boy as big as Jack, grinning all the time
12. Water from the sky
14. Jack paints his with clay
16. Feeling the Littluns had
17. An animal man
18. The bodies of Simon and the parachutist are carried out to _____
19. Shell, symbol of authority
22. Jack announces to Ralph, I'm not going to _____ anymore. Not with you.
24. It had to be collected to burn
25. Sam and Eric see the _____ of a parachutist
28. The boys' _____ grew long
30. Thickly wooded area
32. The boys use Piggy's _____ to start the fire
35. Author
36. The boys used the _____'s rays to start a fire
37. Castle _____
38. Conceal
39. Choir leader, ugly without silliness
40. Jack does this when he lifts his knife to kill the piglet

DOWN

1. Boys' transportation to the island
2. Name given to the numerous little children of the group
3. Sam and Eric; identical twins
4. Place from which the boys see something like a great ape
5. Another name for leader
6. _____ of the Flies
7. The choir boys become this; responsible for getting food
8. Jack plans to steal it from Ralph and Piggy
9. A snake-thing in the forest
10. The hunters' _____ was the act of killing
13. Sob
15. Maurice and Roger destroy the Littluns' sand _____
16. Shape of the rock on which Piggy lands
18. Poetic, sensitive, loner, mysterious boy
20. A British naval _____saves Ralph
21. Simon falls off one to the sands below
23. Man vs. man, for example
26. Intelligent, reader and thinker rather than a boy of action
27. Expression on pig's face
29. Handsome, athletic, natural leader
31. Ralph encounters a grinning pig's
33. Pointed stick
34. Symbolic of evil
35. _____ vs. evil
36. Roger stalks Henry and throws these near him

CROSSWORD ANSWER KEY - *Lord of the Flies*

```
. . . . . A D U L T S . M . C A N D L E . .
. H . . . I . I . A . . O . H . . . . O F .
B O U L D E R . T . M A U R I C E . R A I N .
E . N A . P . . T . N . N E . F A C E . F E A R
A . T . L . . . U . R A . . . A . . L . . . Y
S . E . C . . . N . R I . . . S A V A G E . .
T . R . E . . . N . I I . C O N C H . T . T .
I . S . S E A S . . S . . . F . L . P L A Y . C
E . . . . I . . . . . . . F . I . . E . W O O D
. . . . . M . . . . . F . F . G . . . . . N .
. . . C O R P S E . . . I . F G . . . . . F .
H A I R . N . I . . . . C . F O R E S T . F .
. . . A . . . G L A S S E S . I . K . D . L .
. G O L D I N G . P . R . S U N . U . A . I .
. O . . . Y . E . R . T . . . L . R O C K .
. O . H I D E . J A C K . O . . L . K . T .
. D . . . . . R . . . N . . . . . N . . . .
. . . . . . . . . H E S I T A T E S . . . .
. . . . . . . . . S . . . . . . S . . . .
. . . . . . . . . . . . . . . S . . . . .
```

109

MATCHING QUIZ/WORKSHEET 1 - *Lord of the Flies*

___ 1. LITTLUNS

A. Sob

___ 2. GOOD

B. Author

___ 3. RALPH

C. The bodies of Simon and the parachutist are carried out to

___ 4. RAIN

D. A British naval _____ saves Ralph

___ 5. PIGGY

E. Water from the sky

___ 6. GOLDING

F. Intelligent, reader and thinker rather than a boy of action

___ 7. FEAR

G. Name given to the numerous little children of the group

___ 8. CRY

H. Choir leader, ugly without silliness

___ 9. SEA

I. Ralph encounters a grinning pig's _____

___ 10. HAIR

J. Pointed stick

___ 11. SPEAR

K. Conceal

___ 12. HIDE

L. An animal man

___ 13. SAMNERIC

M. Feeling the Littluns had

___ 14. SAVAGE

N. Sam and Eric; identical twins

___ 15. JACK

O. Jack criticizes the boys for their lack of this

___ 16. COOPERATION

P. The boys' _____ grew long

___ 17. SKULL

Q. Simon falls off one to the sands below

___ 18. CLIFF

R. The boys use Piggy's _____ to start the fire

___ 19. GLASSES

S. _____ vs. evil

___ 20. OFFICER

T. Handsome, athletic, natural leader

MATCHING QUIZ/WORKSHEET 2 - *Lord of the Flies*

___ 1. HUNTERS   A. Jack plans to steal it from Ralph and Piggy

___ 2. SUN   B. Shell, symbol of authority

___ 3. CHIEF   C. Name given to the numerous little children of the group

___ 4. COOPERATION   D. The choir boys become this; responsible for getting food

___ 5. DANCE   E. The hunters' _____ was the act of killing

___ 6. FEAR   F. Feeling the Littluns had

___ 7. RALPH   G. Another name for leader

___ 8. CONCH   H. There are no _____ on the island until the officer arrives

___ 9. SIMON   I. The boys used the _____'s rays to start a fire

___ 10. CRY   J. A British naval _____ saves Ralph

___ 11. LORD   K. Jack does this when he lifts his knife to kill the piglet

___ 12. SKULL   L. Handsome, athletic, natural leader

___ 13. OFFICER   M. _____ of the Flies

___ 14. RAIN   N. Poetic, sensitive, loner, mysterious boy

___ 15. HESITATES   O. Jack criticizes the boys for their lack of this

___ 16. PIGGY   P. Intelligent, reader and thinker rather than a boy of action

___ 17. STONES   Q. Roger stalks Henry and throws these near him

___ 18. LITTLUNS   R. Water from the sky

___ 19. FIRE   S. Sob

___ 20. ADULTS   T. Ralph encounters a grinning pig's _____

KEY: MATCHING QUIZ/WORKSHEETS - *Lord of the Flies*

Worksheet 1	Worksheet 2
1. G	1. D
2. S	2. I
3. T	3. G
4. E	4. O
5. F	5. E
6. B	6. F
7. M	7. L
8. A	8. B
9. C	9. N
10. P	10. S
11. J	11. M
12. K	12. T
13. N	13. J
14. L	14. R
15. H	15. K
16. O	16. P
17. I	17. Q
18. Q	18. C
19. R	19. A
20. D	20. H

SCRAMBLED	WORD	CLUE
OFICCTNL	CONFLICT	Man vs. man, for example
IUNTMONA	MOUNTAIN	Place from which the boys see something like a great ape
FECFORI	OFFICER	A British naval _____ saves Ralph
NSU	SUN	The boys used the _____'s rays to start a fire
ESTLCA	CASTLE	Maurice and Roger destroy the littluns' sand _____
MNOIS	SIMON	Poetic, sensitive, loner, mysterious boy
AFTL	FLAT	Shape of the rock on which Piggy lands
YCR	CRY	Sob
ULDEBRO	BOULDER	It shatters the conch and Piggy
OSFTER	FOREST	Thickly wooded area
UCMIERA	MAURICE	Choir boy as big as Jack, grinning all the time
CEDAN	DANCE	The hunters' _____ was the act of killing
DRLO	LORD	_____ of the Flies
IGNR	GRIN	Expression on pig's face
CHOCN	CONCH	Shell, symbol of authority
ODWO	WOOD	It had to be collected to burn
ERFA	FEAR	Feeling the Littluns had
AEFC	FACE	Jack paints his with clay
LDCNEA	CANDLE	Jack slashed the green _____ buds
ASE	SEA	The bodies of Simon and the parachutist are carried out to _____
CJKA	JACK	Choir leader, ugly without silliness
LYPA	PLAY	Jack announces to Ralph, I'm not going to _____ anymore, not with you.
FFCLI	CLIFF	Simon falls off one to the sands below
ITHSTEESA	HESITATES	Jack does this when he lifts his knife to kill the piglet
LIGONGD	GOLDING	Author
AEGSLSS	GLASSES	The boys use Piggy's _____ to start the fire
SONSTE	STONES	Roger stalks Henry and throws these near him
NOSMI	SIMON	Poetic, sensitive, loner, mysterious boy
RLIEAPAN	AIRPLANE	Boys' transportation to the island
DEIH	HIDE	Conceal
UNRSHET	HUNTERS	The choir boys become this; responsible for getting food
ARNI	RAIN	Water from the sky
EFIR	FIRE	Jack plans to steal it from Ralph and Piggy

VOCABULARY RESOURCE MATERIALS

VOCABULARY WORD SEARCH - *Lord of the Flies*

All words in this list are associated with *Lord of the Flies* with an emphasis on the vocabulary words chosen for study in the text. The words are placed backwards, forward, diagonally, up and down. The included words are listed below.

```
D E C L I V I T I E S I N E W Y Z G R D P Y M W
M F X L C O W V C M R N R O L S N P E J R Y H P
X C G K G Q B N N S P W O G I I U T V G O L Z N
N X K L S X A T Q J L E N I T T A O T P T W X V
S A N C T I T Y U L C I R A T L S H I A T U S G
M H K K R E T P A S T R L V U A S A T C Z J G S
R K K U U K P N T A E I T C I M T F B V E G V S
Y F X Q R Y R N I L M N I X S O N N F G D P E D
T U A J C E R C E I J T E I H I U S A E E L S Y
L P L Q T T U P S D S Y C S M X V S N C C H Y B
O V M A R R H S E E L I C P S D F O N A N S T X
T D M B C A A S G T N C A V M E O E N Q T I V B
H G P X N E P Y N Y N L D H V T I N Y R I C W W
C P E T L I K E C G P S L I S L I K E N L J X Y
Q Y I V L D L U T A H E S E L P P V I V B K L D
I N S C R U T A B L E I F U R U O M A L G T E L
E F E M C P U L P E R B B F R C I D M Y I W L X
N Z R U W T E Y G E R E D G I C C C P C E L V B
D E R I S I O N D K X R E B A G M J A K A C C D
Y T I L U D E R C N I D D L R C Y T S P C R Y Z
```

APEX	EFFIGY	INCREDULITY	PURGED
ASSIMILATING	ELEPHANTINE	INIMICAL	REBUKE
BASTION	EXCRUCIATINGLY	INSCRUTABLE	SANCTITY
COVERTS	FESTOONED	LUXURIANCE	SINEWY
CYNICISM	GESTICULATED	MATERNAL	SKEWED
DECLIVITIES	GLAMOUR	MYOPIA	SPECIOUS
DERISION	HIATUS	OBTUSENESS	TACITLY
DERISIVE	IMPALPABLE	OPAQUE	TAUT
EBULLIENCE	IMPERVIOUS	PALL	TRUCULENTLY
ECLIPSED	INCANTATION	PINNACLES	

VOCABULARY CROSSWORD CLUES - *Lord of the Flies*

ACROSS

1. Feeling the Littluns had
3. A well-fortified position
5. A visual defect like nearsightedness
9. Shape of the rock on which Piggy lands
10. A likeness or image
11. Crackling sound
14. Sob
16. A gloomy effect
17. The highest point
18. A break
19. Tight
21. Turned to one side
23. Lean and muscular
25. The boys used the _____'s rays to start a fire
30. Attitude scornful of the motives or virtues of others
31. Light can't get through it
34. Scorn or ridicule
35. Conceal
36. _____ of the Flies
37. The hunters' _____ was the act of killing
38. Poetic, sensitive, loner, mysterious boy
39. The bodies of Simon and the parachutist are carried out to _____
40. Freed from impurities
41. There are no _____ on the island until the officer arrives

DOWN

2. Water from the sky
4. Intangible; not perceived by touch
5. Relating to motherhood
6. Tall, pointed formations
7. Jack announces to Ralph, I'm not going to _____ anymore. Not with you.
8. Roger stalks Henry and throws these near him
10. Ponderously clumsy
11. Thick underbrush providing cover
12. Without being spoken
13. Obscured; blocked from view
15. Magic spell; enchantment
17. Absorbing
20. Downward slopes
22. A verbal charm or spell
24. Zestful enthusiasm
26. Unfriendly; hostile
27. Incapable of being affected
28. Author
29. Decorated
32. Scornful
33. Thickly wooded area

119

Completed crossword grid (· = filled/black square):

```
F E A R · · B A S T I O N · M Y O P I A · P · S
· · A · · · · M · · · A · · I · · · · · F L A T
E F F I G Y · C R E P I T A T I O N · E · A · O
L · N · · · O · A · A · · E · N · C R Y · · · N
E · G · · · V · L · C · · R · F A L L · · · · E
P · · A P E X · P · I · · N · · C · I · · · · S
H I A T U S · R · T A U T · A · · L · P · · · ·
A · M · S · T · B · L · L · · · E · S · D · · ·
N · O · I · S · L · Y · · · · S K E W E D · · ·
T · U · M · E · · · · · · · I · · S · C · · · ·
I · R · S I N E W Y · · · · S U N · I · L · · I
N · G · L · B · · · · F · · C Y N I C I S M · ·
E · O P A Q U E · D · E · · A · I · · V · · · P
· F · L · T · · L · D E R I S I O N · M · H I D E
L O R D · I · L · R · · · T · · I · · T · · · ·
· R · I · N · I · · O · D A N C E · I · V · · ·
· E · N · G · E · · S I M O N · T · A · E · · ·
· S · G · N · · · · I · · N · I · · S · · · · ·
· T · · · C · · V · S E A · O · · · · U · · · ·
· · · P U R G E D · E · D · N · A D U L T S · ·
```

VOCABULARY WORKSHEET 1 - *Lord of the Flies*

_____ 1. Light can't get through it
    A. assimilating B. excruciatingly   C. opaque D. sinewy

_____ 2. Having rich or profuse growth
    A. gesticulated B. luxuriance   C. eclipsed D. impervious

_____ 3. To invent without preparation
    A. pinnacles B. improvisation   C. maternal D. propitatingly

_____ 4. Scornful
    A. cynicism B. obtuseness   C. specious D. derisive

_____ 5. Lean and muscular
    A. derisive B. sinewy   C. obtuseness D. specious

_____ 6. A visual defect like nearsightedness
    A. myopia B. derision   C. luxuriance D. coverts

_____ 7. Intensely painfully
    A. derisive B. excruciatingly   C. myopia D. ebullience

_____ 8. Dullness; flatness; lack of sharp edges
    A. crepitation B. obtuseness   C. festooned D. maternal

_____ 9. Tall, pointed formations
    A. pinnacles B. pall   C. maternal D. apex

_____ 10. A gloomy effect
    A. derision B. inscrutable   C. specious D. pall

_____ 11. Plausible but actually false
    A. pinnacles B. pall   C. derision D. specious

_____ 12. Without being spoken
    A. ebullience B. declivities   C. tacitly D. tempestuously

_____ 13. Ponderously clumsy
    A. impervious B. improvisation   C. elephantine D. myopia

_____ 14. Disbelief
    A. skewed B. obtuseness   C. specious D. incredulity

_____ 15. Thick underbrush providing cover
    A. ebullience B. incredulity   C. coverts D. sinewy

_____ 16. Turned to one side
    A. opaque B. skewed   C. specious D. derision

_____ 17. Impenetrable
    A. pinnacles B. impervious   C. crepitation D. inscrutable

_____ 18. Magic spell; enchantment
    A. derision B. glamour   C. effigy D. incantation

_____ 19. Scorn or ridicule
    A. improvisation B. effigy   C. truculently D. derision

_____ 20. Freed from impurities
    A. skewed B. excruciatingly   C. purged D. sinewy

VOCABULARY WORKSHEET 2 - *Lord of the Flies*

___ 1. EFFIGY

A. A verbal charm or spell

___ 2. TRUCULENTLY

B. To invent without preparation

___ 3. CYNICISM

C. Lean and muscular

___ 4. INSCRUTABLE

D. Made hand motions

___ 5. OBTUSENESS

E. Impenetrable

___ 6. GESTICULATED

F. Appeasingly; trying to please

___ 7. BASTION

G. Obscured; blocked from view

___ 8. TACITLY

H. A well-fortified position

___ 9. INIMICAL

I. Like a storm; turbulently

___ 10. IMPROVISATION

J. Attitude scornful of the motives or virtues of others

___ 11. SINEWY

K. Disposed to fight

___ 12. MATERNAL

L. Tight

___ 13. PROPITATINGLY

M. Dullness; flatness; lack of sharp edges

___ 14. INCANTATION

N. The highest point

___ 15. SANCTITY

O. A likeness or image

___ 16. TAUT

P. Without being spoken

___ 17. ECLIPSED

Q. Sacredness; godliness

___ 18. APEX

R. Unfriendly; hostile

___ 19. CREPITATION

S. Relating to motherhood

___ 20. TEMPESTUOUSLY

T. Crackling sound

KEY: VOCABULARY WORKSHEETS - *Lord of the Flies*

Worksheet 1	Worksheet 2
1. C	1. O
2. B	2. K
3. B	3. J
4. A	4. E
5. B	5. M
6. A	6. D
7. B	7. H
8. B	8. P
9. A	9. R
10. D	10. B
11. D	11. C
12. C	12. S
13. C	13. F
14. D	14. A
15. C	15. Q
16. B	16. L
17. D	17. G
18. D	18. N
19. D	19. T
20. C	20. I

SCRAMBLED	WORD	CLUE
LPLA	PALL	A gloomy effect
OITITNNCNAA	INCANTATION	A verbal charm or spell
IOSSECPU	SPECIOUS	Plausible but actually false
TPRGAPIYNLTOI	PROPITATINGLY	Appeasingly; trying to please
ALTRSECBINU	INSCRUTABLE	Impenetrable
ASTYICFN	SANCTIFY	Sacredness; godliness
UDERPG	PURGED	Freed from impurities
POAITOSIMIRNV	IMPROVISATION	To invent without preparation
EUQPAO	OPAQUE	Light can't get through it
DNOOESFTE	FESTOONED	Decorated
PEXA	APEX	The highest point
MASATLISINGI	ASSIMILATING	Absorbing
YNSIEW	SINEWY	Lean and muscular
ATTU	TAUT	Tight
AENLAMTR	MATERNAL	Relating to motherhood
NESIPNCLA	PINNACLES	Tall, pointed formations
SCINIMCY	CYNICISM	Attitude scornful of the motives or virtues of others
GIFYEF	EFFIGY	A likeness or image
EUKBER	REBUKE	To criticize or reprimand
ECITDLSIEVI	DECLIVITIES	Downward slopes
EWDSKE	SKEWED	Turned to one side
ALUSDECTEGIT	GESTICULATED	Made hand motions
PIMAOY	MYOPIA	A visual defect like nearsightedness
TLYTACI	TACITLY	Without being spoken
NCEULEBLIE	EBULLIENCE	Zestful enthusiasm
SIVDIEER	DERISIVE	Scornful
ELESDCIP	ECLIPSED	Obscured; blocked from view
VCTSERO	COVERTS	Thick underbrush providing cover
UIMVOPSIER	IMPERVIOUS	Incapable of being affected
IPTENLANEHE	ELEPHANTINE	Ponderously clumsy
SUNBESOSET	OBTUSENESS	Dullness; flatness; lacking sharp edges
ETATCNOPRII	CREPITATION	Crackling sound
OSTIBNA	BASTION	A well-fortified position
ACIEUXRLUN	LUXURIANCE	Having rich or profuse growth
YNRUEULTLTC	TRUCULENTLY	Disposed to fight
ILINDRYUECT	INCREDULITY	Disbelief
THIASU	HIATUS	A break